Letter of the Week!

A Reproducible Resource Book for Early Childhood Educators

Author	Christine Clemente Stack
Illustrator	Karen Sevaly
Editorial/Art Director	Karen Sevaly
Graphic Designers	Yvonne McElhenny
	Debbie Schultz

**Look for all Teacher's Friend
Early Childhood Thematic Books and Little Kids Can...Books
at your local school supply store!**

teacher's friend publications

Copyright © 2002
Teacher's Friend, a Scholastic Company.
All rights reserved.
Printed in China.

1 2 3 4 5 6 7 8 9 10   15 14 13 12 11 10 09

**ISBN-13 978-0-439-50407-2
ISBN-10 0-439-50407-4**

Scholastic Inc., 557 Broadway, New York, NY 10012

Table of Contents

About The Author

Christine Clemente Stack is from a suburban community in upstate New York. She holds permanent certification as a Special Education Teacher. As an educator for over twelve years, she has had the opportunity to spend many hours dedicated to the encouragement and enhancement of the development of young children. She has been engaged in several professional opportunities, including teacher, supervisor, presenter/trainer, facilitator, collaborator, mentor, Early Intervention Specialist, and Child Development Specialist. Her most rewarding aspect of each position has been the time spent with children and their families. She encourages you to enjoy this book and hopes that it will help you to better serve each young child in your care.

Safety Warning!

Parents and professionals should use their best judgment to determine whether a particular idea or suggestion would be appropriate to use with an individual child or group of children.

It is important that children only use materials and products labeled child-safe and non-toxic. Small children should always be supervised by a competent adult and youngsters must never be allowed to put small objects or art materials in their mouths. Please consult the manufacturer's safety warnings on all materials and equipment used with young children.

When using food products, make sure that you take into consideration any children's allergies or food restrictions. Make sure that you take special note of the beliefs, values, and culture of the families you serve.

Introduction

This Letter of the Week resource book is full of skill-based ideas that are meant to inspire you to use your own creativity and imagination as you teach young children about the letters (symbols) and the sounds (phonemes) of the English language.

Early communication skills develop into the ability to read and write. Reading is the ability to decode and comprehend written material. Writing is the ability to express ideas, thoughts, knowledge, or information through the use of fine motor skills and writing utensils to combine symbols (pictures, letters, words, and sentences) in a meaningful way. It has often been said "the young child learns to read and older child reads to learn." Books and other written materials carry messages. One needs to master the ability to decode words as well as the ability to understand what the writer is expressing in the text.

The young learner quickly masters all aspects of communication to become a literate individual. Children demonstrate success in literacy (reading and writing) when four pieces are put together (rich vocabulary, letter knowledge, sound knowledge, and fine motor skills). These are essential skills for the young learner because we use literacy every day. The early childhood educator is responsible for building on a rich vocabulary, letter knowledge, sound knowledge, and fine motor skills by providing various types of opportunities to the young learner with consideration to variations in development.

This book provides a wide variety of ideas and activities using the popular words associated with each letter. The ideas for each letter encourage teachers to introduce as many words as possible that start with a particular letter (initial consonant or vowel.) Initial blends (two or three consonants grouped together) can be introduced later as the children progress. When teaching the initial consonants, it is important to know that some letters have one sound (phoneme) (i.e., L, N, P), while other letters represent more than one sound (i.e., A,E, I, O, U, C, G).

This resource book's main focus is to enhance reading readiness skills by enforcing initial consonant knowledge and initial sound knowledge. However, the activities naturally develop a child's language, vocabulary and fine motor skills, as well as incorporate ideas that expose children to mathematical concepts and science properties. The ideas and activities support the child's growth across the five developmental domains (communication, adaptive, motor/physical, cognitive, and social/personal/emotional).

Consider the following letter knowledge and sound knowledge skills when assessing the children before and after implementing the activities:

Letter Knowledge
- ☐ recites the alphabet
- ☐ discriminates between letters and other designs
- ☐ matches letters
- ☐ points to letters when named
- ☐ names letters when pointed to
- ☐ uses invented spelling
- ☐ points to labels in the classroom

☐ recognizes first letter then other letters of name
☐ understands that the letters/words carry the message
☐ reads some words by sight

Sound Knowledge
☐ listens
☐ produces different sounds
☐ participates in rhyming games and fingerplays
☐ discriminates between letter sounds
☐ recognizes different letter sounds
☐ matches sounds to pictures
☐ makes connection between sound and symbol

Each child will obtain these concepts and skills at their own rate. The teacher's role is to facilitate the learning of these concepts by engaging the children in activities and conversations about letters and sounds and their relationship to words in the English language. Teachers should utilize natural opportunities to point out letters/words and their sounds in the environment, as well as plan activities that emphasize particular letters or sounds.

The classroom should be "print-rich" and letters and words should be apparent throughout the classroom. For example, the early childhood classroom should include:

• Relevant books in every center
• Texture letters - magnetic, felt, foam, sandpaper, cookie cutter letters, etc.
• Labels in every center that are pointed out in a meaningful manner
• Materials labeled
• Real product packages and containers placed in the relevant center
• Signs for centers and materials
• Typical items that have letters or words on them (i.e., telephone book and recipe cards in the Dramatic Play Center or maps and street signs in the Building and Block Center)
• A variety of writing materials and writing tools in each center

How to Use This Book

This resource book includes an array of ideas, skill-based activities and reproducible pages that you as an early childhood educator can utilize to develop stimulating experiences around a given letter/sound. The letter pages, picture cards, game ideas and other reproducible pages throughout the book are meant to be copied for individual classroom use. You may adapt or modify the ideas or instructions to best meet the developmental level of the children you serve. As a time saver, protect your work by laminating the products or by placing the reproducible pages in plastic page protectors. The following describes each section and offers some helpful tips and hints regarding how to implement the ideas into your curriculum:

Children's Alphabet Literature List – This list of children's literature emphasizes the alphabet and beginning sounds/letters. It includes books to read aloud, picture books, and books for beginning readers.

A Few Ideas for All Letters - This section includes ideas and activities that can be completed with each letter/sound.

Manuscript Letters – The manuscript alphabet depicted on this page will assist you the teacher (or parent) in teaching the correct formation and direction of the written letters.

Letter Pages - Each letter "chapter" includes the following sections:

Uppercase and Lowercase Letter Symbols - Copy the letter pages at the beginning of each letter chapter (enlarge them if necessary). Have the children cover the letter with something that starts with the letter. Here are a few ideas:

A – acorns, apple seeds	**I** – Ivory Snowflakes	**Q** – Q-tips®, quarters (plastic)
B – beans (dry), buttons	**J** – jewels	**R** – rubber bands **Y** – yellow yarn
C – corks, crayons, cotton balls	**K** – kidney beans (dry)	**S** – stones, seeds
D – dots (stickers)	**L** - leaves	**T** – tissue paper **Z** – "z" from
E – egg shells	**M** - macaroni	**U** – "u" from magazines magazines
F – feathers, felt	**N** – nut shells	**V** – velour/velvet pieces
G – gold glitter	**O** – oatmeal (dry)	**W** – wallpaper, watermelon seeds
H – hearts (small punched)	**P** - paperclips	**X** – "x" from magazines

The letter patterns can also be used to make "touchy-feely" letters, such as letters cut from sandpaper, felt, or wallpaper. Instruct the children to trace the "textured" letters with their fingers (tracing should be instructed in the same way as children are taught to write the letters).

Ideas and Activities for Each Letter – Designate a special time of day for the "Letter of the Week" activities. Make sure that the activities emphasize words beginning with the chosen letter. Teach one letter sound at a time. Some letters, such as "c" and "g," make more than one sound. Use the ideas as a supplement to your phonemic awareness/phonics curriculum. The ideas are organized in alphabetical order and span the various developmental skills of young learners.

Educators will discover that the ideas and activities can be utilized in the traditional early childhood centers [Arts and Crafts, Music and Movement, Blocks and Building, Library and Writing, Dramatic Play, Cooking and Nutrition, Math and Manipulatives (Science)] and during activity times (group/circle time, snack/lunch, free play/work time, gross motor/outside time, transition activity). Throughout the book, you will notice a "Home Activity" symbol. These activities can be completed either during school time or can be sent home to parents via newsletters or notes. An important element to a child's success in school is the encouragement and participation of the parents.

A Note About Blends - Initial letters should be introduced to children before words that begin with two consonant sounds, commonly known as blends. Blend sounds should only be introduced after the initial sounds are mastered. For example, before you introduce "br," both the "b" and the "r" sound should have been mastered. In the case of consonant combinations that make a "new" phoneme (sound), such as "ch" or "ph," the new sound should be introduced separate from both the individual sounds.

Picture Cards - These cute illustrations can be used in a number of ways. Here are just a few suggestions:

Construct a simple matching game by making two copies (using heavy paper) and cutting them apart. The children turn the cards over and try to find the matches.

Make a simple sound sorting game by taking pictures from two different letters and asking the children to sort them by their first letter/sound. For example, copy the "B" and "P" letter/word cards and have the children look at each picture, say its name and place it in either the "B" or "P" pile.

Display the picture cards with the matching word cards on the classroom bulletin board. (Not all pictures cards come with a matching word card. In this case, make your own using standard index cards.) An activity for older children can also be made using the cards. Instruct them to match the appropriate picture and word cards together.

In addition, the cards represent long and short vowel sounds. Copy several picture card sets and ask the children to sort them by short vowel sound. Start with two vowels, then include cards representing three or more vowels. Or use cards that represent the long and short sounds of one vowel (i.e., long and short "a"). Ask the children to sort them into two lunch bags, demonstrating how they can discriminate between the two sounds. Or develop sentences or stories using cards and words from one or more vowel group.

Some of the cards include pictures that begin with initial blends. As mentioned earlier, blends should be taught after initial consonants are introduced. Blends either combine two sounds together or they represent their own sound. The picture cards can be used to make matching games or in sound sorting activities.

Word Cards - These word cards can be used to match with the picture cards, label items in the classroom, or used in an "Explore Tub." Create an Explore Tub by using an empty water table, a large box, or a laundry basket. Collect the "real" items on the word cards. And then tape the word cards to the matching item. Allow the children to explore the items. The teacher can point out the word (emphasizing the initial sound) and then have the children repeat the word. Some children may be able to tell you each letter in the word.

Trace and Write - Encourage the children to use this page to practice writing the letters using correct form.

My Alphabet Book - This reproducible page reinforces the skills learned by providing practice for the child in writing the letters correctly. Children can also write simple words that begin with the chosen letter and draw a picture of an object that represents the letter of the week. At the end of the year, have the children assemble them in alphabetical order and attach them together in a binder or staple them into a student-made book.

Children's Alphabet Literature List

Archambault, John, et al., **Chicka Chicka Boom Boom.** Aladdin Books, 2000

Beller, Janet. **A-B-C-ing: An Action Alphabet.** Crown, 1984

Boynton, Sandra. **A is for Angry: An Animal and Adjective Alphabet.** Children's Press, 1983

Brown, Deni. **My Little ABC Board Book, My First Books.** Dorling Kindersley Publishing, Inc., 1998

Cleary, Beverly. **The Hullabaloo ABC.** William Morrow Co., 1998

Crosbie, Michael, **Arches to Zig Zags: An Architecture ABC.** Harry N. Abrams, 2000

Dragonwagon, Crescent. **Alligator Arrived with Apples: A Potluck Alphabet Feast.** Aladdin Paperbacks, 1992

Dr. Seuss. **Dr. Seuss's ABC, I Can Read It All By Myself Beginner Book.** Random House Books For Young Readers, 1996

Edwards, Pamela D. **The Wacky Wedding: A Book of Alphabet Antics.** Hyperion Press, 1999

Ehlert, Lois. **Eating the Alphabet: Fruits and Vegetables From A to Z.** Harcourt Trade Publishers, 1996

Eichenberg, Fritz. **Ape in A Cape: An Alphabet of Odd Animals.** Harcourt Children's Books, 1988

Grover, Max. **The Accidental Zucchini: An Unexpected Alphabet.** Harcourt Brace, 1997

Gustafson, Scott. **Alphabet Soup: A Feast of Letters.** Greenwich Workshop Press, 1996

Hausman, Bonnie. **A to Z-Do You Ever Feel Like Me?: A Guessing Alphabet of Feelings, Words, and Other Cool Stuff.** Dutton Books, 1999

Johnson, Audean. **A to Z Look and See.** Random House, 1986

Johnson, Stephen, T., **Alphabet City.** Penguin Group, 1999

Lionni, Leo. **The Alphabet Tree.** Alfred A Knopf Books For Young Readers, 1990

Lynch, Wayne. **Arctic Alphabet: Exploring The North From A to Z.** Firefly Books Limited, 1999

Micklethwait, Lucy. **I Spy: An Alphabet in Art.** William Morrow & Co., 1996

Shannon, George. **Tomorrow's Alphabet.** William Morrow & Co., 1999

Sierra, Judy. **There's a Zoo in Room 22.** Harcourt, 2000

Slate, Joseph. **Miss Bindergarten Gets Ready for Kindergarten.** Penguin Putnam, 2001

Tabor, Nancy Grande. **Albertina Anda Arriba.** Charlesbridge Publishing, Inc., 1993

Van Allsburg, Chris. **The Z was Zapped.** Houghton Mifflin, 1998

Viorst, Judith. **The Alphabet from Z to A: With Much Confusion On The Way.** Atheneum, 1994

Wood, Audrey. **Alphabet Adventure.** Scholastic, Inc., 2001

A Few Ideas for All Letters

Keep a Word Board

Carry 3x5 index cards in your pocket. As you engage in activities that emphasize the letter of the week, write the word on the index card. Display the cards on a classroom board with the heading "These Words Begin With the Letter _____." Start your word board using the names of children in your class that start with the chosen letter. (Children are always very interested in their names and the letters in their names. First and last names are the first words most children learn to sound out and write.)

Classroom Letter Collage

In this activity, the class works together or in groups of 4 to 5 children per letter shape. Cut out a large shape of the letter of the week. The children cut or tear out pictures of things that start with that letter/sound or the letter itself. They glue the pictures, letters, or real items that start with the letter onto the large letter to create a classroom letter collage. Display the finished creation on the class board.

Where in the World?

Introduce children to geography by using a globe or map. Find streets/cities/states/countries/seas that begin with the letter of the week. Each time you look at the map or globe, start by pointing out where you are and then find a few locations that start with the given letter. Write the words on the word board or on a separate paper with the heading "Where In The World?"

Alphabet Games

Encourage the children to play one of these alphabet games after they have mastered the sounds of several letters.

Going On A Picnic – Sit the children in a circle and instruct each child to name an item they would like to take on a picnic that begins with the letter of the week or with one of the letters they have recently learned. As you proceed around the circle, each child must name all of the items mentioned before adding their own. For example, the first child says: "I'm going on a picnic and I'm going to take an apple." The second child says: "I'm going on a picnic and I'm going to take an apple and an alligator."

Alphabet Catch – Have the children sit in a circle. Choose one child to stand in the center and toss a soft ball or bean bag to someone in the circle. While tossing, the "tosser" calls out a letter of the alphabet. The "catcher" must answer with a word that begins with that letter. If the "catcher" answers correctly, he/she can stay in the circle. If the answer is incorrect, the "catcher" must sit outside of the circle until the next round.

Manuscript Alphabet

Letter A

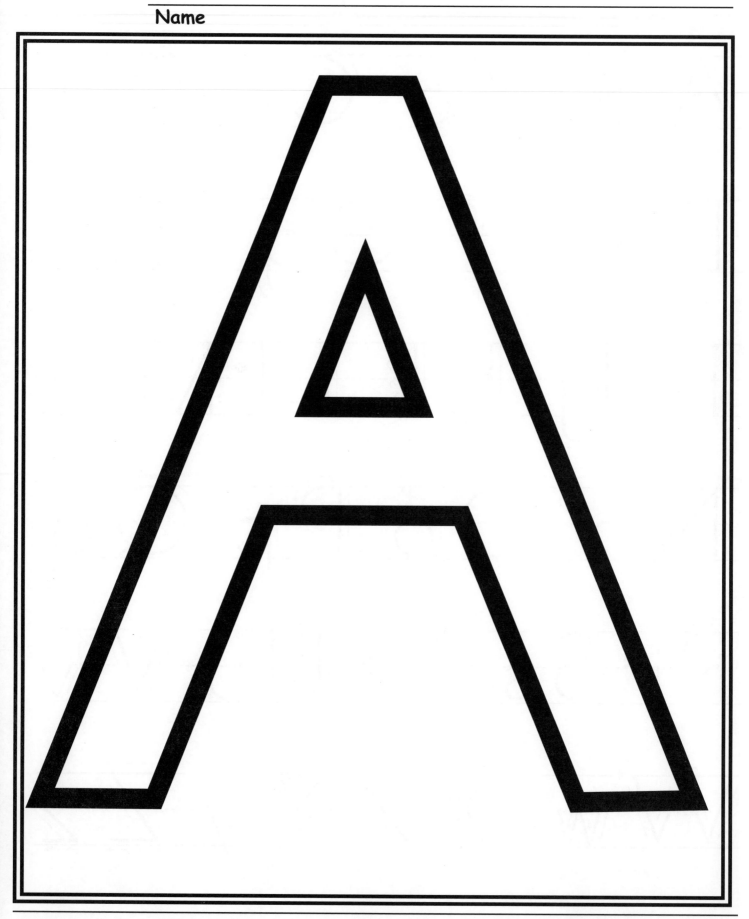

Letter a

Name

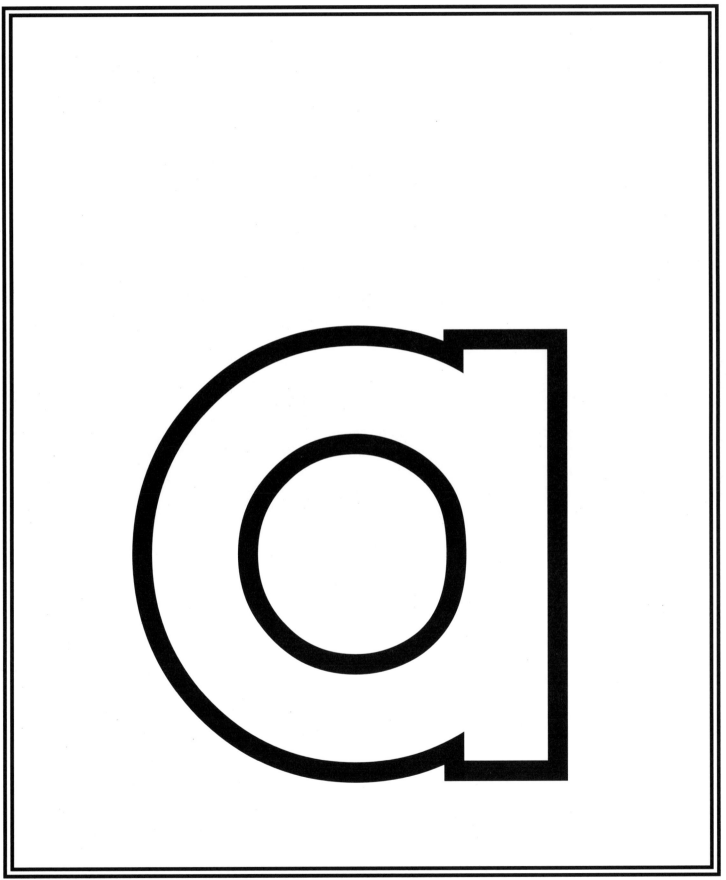

Ideas and Activities for the Letter:

Aardvark, Alligator, Armadillo, and Ape
Learn about animals that start with the letter "a" (including: **aardvark, alligator, armadillo, and ape**). What do they look like? Where do they live? How do they move around? What do they eat? Are they dangerous?

Accordion
Invite an older student who can play the **accordion** to the classroom to demonstrate how it sounds, what it looks like, and how to play it.

Acorn
Tell the children that **acorns** are "the nut of the oak tree." Squirrels and other small animals collect them in the **autumn** to eat throughout the winter months. In the autumn, take the children outside to collect acorns. Instruct the children to explore them, to count them, press them into play dough or clay, or use them to make an autumn collage (include leaves, twigs and pine cones).

Acrobat
Talk about **acrobats** - people who perform gymnastics (somersaults, flips, walking on balance beams, swinging on bars). Watch a short video of acrobatics/gymnastics (tape a short section of this type of sports event shown on TV). Talk about the different ways that they can move, how much practice they have to do before they can do a complete routine, and how important it is that there is a coach and spotter working with them so that they don't get injured.

Action
Ask the children: "How many **actions** can you do with your "A" body parts?" (**ankles, arms**). Make a list and practice them.

Actor/Actress
Tell the children that actors/actresses are people whose job it is to perform or act for other people. They may perform on a stage (play/theater), in a movie, or in a television show. They are usually pretending to be someone else. Sometimes they wear costumes. Brainstorm a list of **actors** and **actresses**. Write their names on a large sheet of paper.

Address
Tell the children that every family has a different address. Your address is the name and number of the place where you live/sleep. Having different addresses helps people (like the mailman) find your home. Copy the house shape (page 16). Write each child's **address** on the lines provided (one address per house). Use the houses for a transition activity.

When the children are lining up, have them tell their address or have the teacher state the addresses one at a time and the children line up as they recognize their address. Display the addresses on a board in your room or by their cubbies or coat hooks.

Afraid
Read a story about being **afraid**. Talk about different times or things that might be scary or make one feel afraid. Talk about how your body reacts when you are afraid. Talk about things the children can do when they are afraid.

Airport/Airplanes
Visit a local **airport** and watch the **airplanes** in the **air**. Learn about the many people who work at an airport. Play with airplanes in the Blocks and Building Center. Play pretend airport in the Dramatic Play Center (include items such as foam trays, chairs in a row, suitcases, tickets, luggage tags).

Album
Make a classroom **album**. Purchase a photo album at a local discount store. Take pictures through-out the year (pictures of the children playing and listening, pictures from field trips and other special events). Insert the pictures in order into the album. Write captions under each picture.

Alike
Make a list on a large sheet of paper of ways or things that make us all **alike**. Examples: We all have two eyes, two legs, two ears, two arms, etc. We all have people that love us. All of us have feelings. We are in Kindergarten (or grade/classroom by teacher's name). We are in school today. We all are learning about...... All of us live in (name of town/city).

Alphabet
Recite the ABC song and read alphabet books. Learn about things that are organized in **alphabetical** order. Examples: telephone book, dictionary, card catalog, files, CDs in a record store, books in a bookstore, attendance list, etc.

Aluminum Foil/Aluminum Cans
Cut **aluminum foil** into small squares. Copy the letter "A" (page 10). Instruct the children to glue the foil squares onto the "A" sheet. Collect **aluminum cans** and donate the refund money to a charitable group or organization. Ask the children to vote on the organization to receive the refund money. Learn about what will happen, not only to the aluminum cans that will be recycled, but also to the money that they donated.

Angle
Have the children trace and then cut along various angle lines that you have drawn on sheets of colored paper.

Angry

Read "That Makes Me **Angry**" by Anthony Best, Western Publishing Co., 1989 or another book about feeling angry. Talk about feeling **angry**. Talk about different times or things that might make one feel angry. Talk about how your body reacts when you are angry. Talk about things the children can do when they are angry that will make them feel better.

Antler

Learn about **animals** with **antlers**. Antlers are the solid horns on top of an animal"s head (sometimes they look like tree branches). Examples: reindeer, deer, moose, and giraffes.

Appetizers

Have a special snack of **"A" appetizers**. Discuss with the children what an appetizer is (a small snack served before a meal, such as dinner). Explain that the portions are usually small, just a taste of the food. Serve the items from a large table, displaying the names of each food by the plate or bowl. Serve a few of the following foods: **alfalfa** sprouts, **almonds**, **alphabet** (cereal or soup), **apples, angel** food **cake, apricots, animal** crackers, **asparagus, American** cheese, or **avocados**.

Apples

Wash and count **apples**. Go **apple** picking. Make **applesauce** or other apple treats. Cut apples in half (find the star) and count apple seeds. Paint with half of any apple by poking a fork into the skin side of the apple. Dip the inside flat part of the apple into paint and then use it to stamp on colored construction paper.

Apricot

Spread **apricot** preserves onto a toasted English muffin to make apricot muffins.

Aquarium

Tell the children that an **aquarium** is a place where animals and plants that live in the water are kept and watched by people. Set up a simple aquarium in your classroom or visit a large aquarium. Children will learn about water creatures and how to care for them.

Arm

Have the children measure the length of their **arms** from fingertip to fingertip across their backs. Then, measure their heights from head to toe. The children will be interested to know that the two numbers should be approximately the same.

Armor
Talk about **animals** with **armor** – a protective covering. Why do they have armor? What is their armor made out of? Examples: **armadillos**, clams, lobsters, turtles, crabs, scallops, beetles, scorpions, crayfish, and snails.

Astronaut
Learn all about **astronauts**. Tell the children that astronauts are people who travel in space in spacecrafts. Look for interesting information on the following website: www.spacecamp.com

Atlas
Bring in an **atlas** to share with the class. Talk about what type of information can be found in an atlas. Can anyone find a state that begins with "**A**"?

Attic
Read the story "What's Up In The **Attic**?" by Liza Alexander, Western Publishing Company Inc., 1987 or another book about the wonderful things that one can find in an attic. Ask the children to go into their **attic** (if they have one) with an **adult** (family member) and write a list of things found in their attic for a home activity.

Auditorium
Go to an event in a school **auditorium**. Explain that the people watching the event are in the **audience** and when the event is over everyone **applauds**. If the event is a play, then inquire about the children meeting the **actors/actresses**.

Aunt
Make an **Awesome Aunt Award**. Provide copies of award patterns and place them in your Library/Writing Center. The children may choose to make a special award for an aunt.

Author
Tell the children that **authors** are people who write books. Keep a running list of names of authors of books read to the class. Post the list in the Library/Writing Center.

Automobile
Tell the children that **automobile** is another name for car. While taking a walk, count the number of automobiles parked on a street or in a parking lot. Play with automobiles in the Blocks and Building Center.

Autumn
Make a list of the different ways animals and people prepare for the winter during the **autumn** months (i.e., gather food, find shelter, clean their yards (leaves), close swimming pools, put summer-time outside toys away, sort through clothes (warm to cold weather), plant bulbs for the spring).

Avenue
Display a local map. Find all of the "avenues." Write a list or circle the names on the map.

Other words that begin with the letter A:
These words may arise in naturally occurring conversations throughout the day/week. As you use these words, point out that they start with the letter "a" and write them on an index card to add to your word board.

above (something high up over one's head)
accident (something getting spilled/broken or someone getting hurt, but not on purpose)
afternoon (time)
ace (in a deck of cards)
age (in relation to a birthday celebration)
ambulance (ambulance siren, safety vehicle)
apartment (some children may live in apartments)
apologize (when a child hurts another child)
April, August (months)
apron (worn during cooking)
assist/assistant (when someone helps someone else)

My name is:

_____

_____

My address is:

_____

_____

_____

Picture Cards

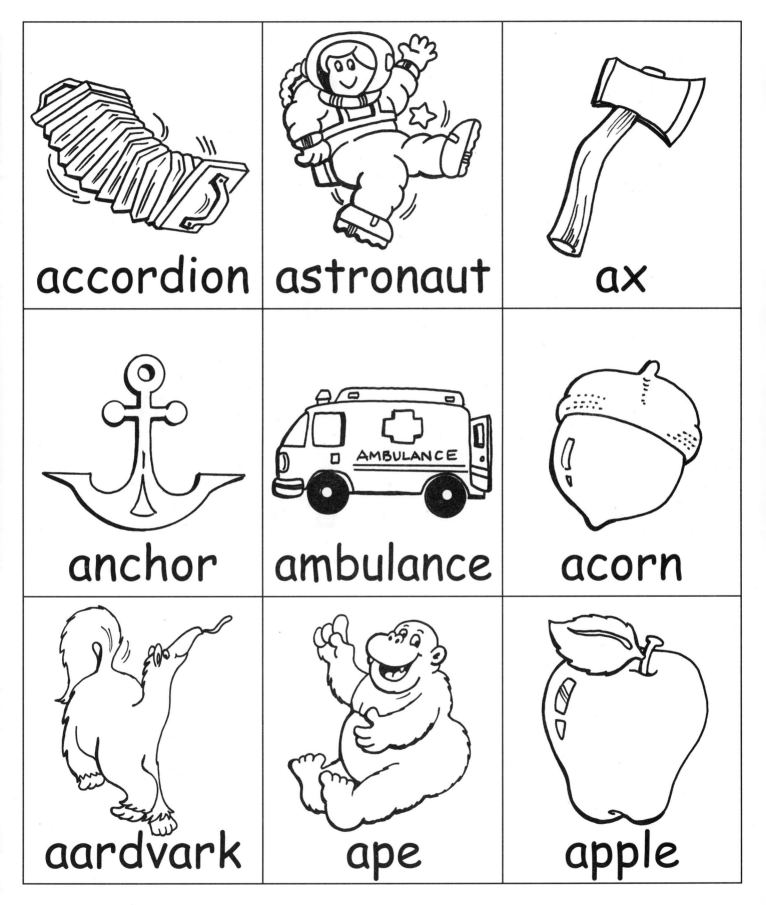

accordion | astronaut | ax

anchor | ambulance | acorn

aardvark | ape | apple

Word Cards

ant farm	ace
accordion	airplane
apple	apron
aquarium	aluminum foil
avocado	atlas
acorn	almond
angel	alligator
ambulance	album

Trace and Write

Trace and write the letters. Color the picture.

Name _____

Uppercase A

A A A A A A A A

Lowercase a

a a a a a a

My Alphabet Book

Name _____

I am learning about the letter A a.
This is how I write it:

A A

a a

Here are some words that start with the letter A a:

This is my picture of an _____ .

Letter B

Name

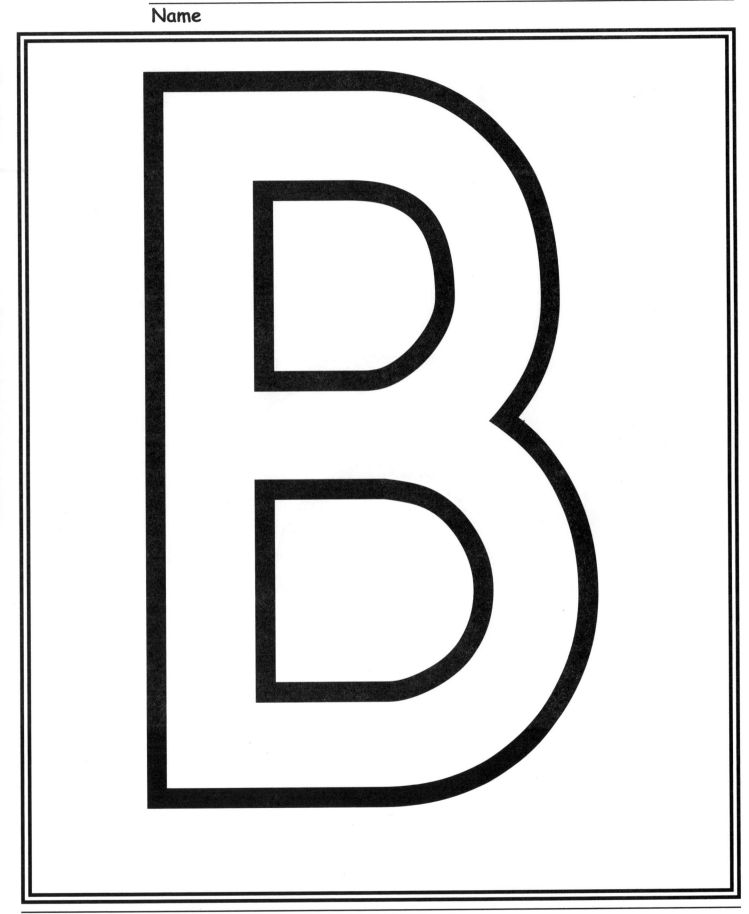

TF1432 *Letter of the Week!*

Letter b

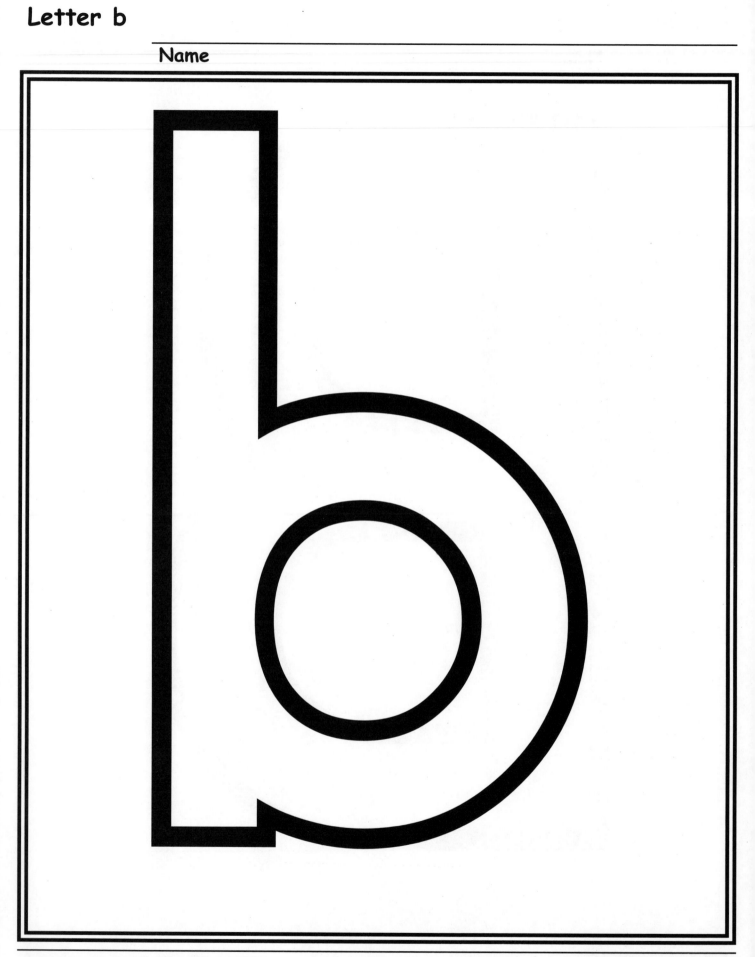

Ideas and Activities for the Letter:

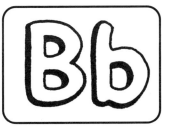

Baby

Invite children to bring in their **baby** pictures to share with their classmates. Have the children guess whose picture it is. Have the children tell something they remember about when they were younger. Talk about **babies**, what they are like and how they are cared
for. Place baby dolls and baby items (clothes, **bottles**, **blankets**, diapers, rocking chair) in the
Dramatic Play Center for pretend play.

Backwards

Invite the children to do some activities **backwards**. (i.e., walk backwards, eat dessert before
lunch, conduct circle backwards-start with activity and end with good morning song, sing the "ABC
song" backwards-zyx, read "The Alphabet From Z to A" by Judith Viorst).

Bag

Collect different sized paper **bags** from retail and grocery stores. Talk about what bags are used
for and the different items that come in different sized bags.

Bagel

Enjoy **bagels** with a variety of toppings. Provide a bagel for each child. Allow the children to choose
their toppings and spread them on with a plastic knife. Topping ideas: peanut **butter**, jelly, **butter**,
or cream cheese.

Baker/Bakery

Visit a local **baker** in a **bakery** shop or the bakery section of a grocery store. Learn about what
bakers do, what types of equipment they use, what types of food they make, and how they display
their food for sale to customers. Play pretend Bakery Shop in the Dramatic Play Center (include
items such as aprons, chef hats, cake pans, cookie sheets, muffin tins, cash register, play food,
spatulas, rolling pin, pie pan, loaf pan, empty bakery ingredient packages, measuring cups/spoons,
signs – name of bake shop, menu of items for sales and their prices).

C, practice walking across a balance beam or piece of wood laid flat on the ground.

... throw, bounce, roll, toss and balance balls. Have the children play by themselves or take turns. Try some balancing activities with large playground balls. For example: sit on the ball and learn how to roll it; hold the ball between your legs and try to walk, hold a ball over your head and drop it... play catch; lay on your belly with your feet up; walk and roll the ball, and ... balance a ball on a blanket... don't let it fall off!

... Put banana slices on top of frozen yogurt. Or use a food dehydrator to make banana chips. This activity demonstrates how food changes under different conditions. Children can ...

Banner

Make a **beautiful** class **banner** to celebrate an upcoming classroom/school event. Have each child add words or pictures, and his or her signature to the banner.

Barbecue

Invite families for a **barbecue**. Serve **burgers**, banana fruit **salad, baked beans, berry** juice and **brownies**. The children can make the salad and brownies. They can make tablecloths for each table by using paints with "B" cookie cutters or sponges on craft/bulletin board paper.

Barber

Set up a **barber shop** in your Dramatic Play Center. Include items such as hairdryer – with cord removed, **brush**, comb, hair pick, non-hair cutting safety scissors, empty shampoo/hairspray **bottles**, barber's smocks, rollers, cash register/money, magazines of different hairstyles (your hairdresser may be willing to donate her/his old hairdressing magazines/books to your program), and sign with prices for each type of service (i.e, haircut, perm, hair coloring, bread trim, shampoo and style, etc.

Bare Feet

Little **bare feet** love to walk and splash in cool water and walk in dry or moist sand. Walk outside in puddles, a stream, or at a local **beach**. Fill a wading pool with water or sand. You may want to have the children paint with bare feet on large sheets of paper. Contact paper can be used to create a sticky surface. Cut a large piece of contact paper, tape it sticky side up on the floor, and allow the children to walk all over the paper with their clean bare feet. Contact paper can be found at a local discount, craft, or teaching supply store.

Bead

String wooden/plastic **beads**. Make patterns using colored beads. Make your own beads by rolling clay into balls. Place the balls onto knitting needles until dry. Paint the beads and, when dry, string them into necklaces or **bracelets**.

Bean

Fill a **box** or your sand/water table with dry **beans** for a change. Add scoops, **bottles** and **bowls**, shovels, and spoons. The children will fill, dump, transfer, sort, and count beans at their own pace.

Blue

The color **blue** can be emphasized in the classroom in several ways. Fill a box with blue items to explore. Make and eat **blueberry** muffins. Paint with blue finger paint. Dye the water in the water table blue. Play with blue play dough. Make a blue collage (include scraps of blue tissue paper, construction paper, yarn, pipe cleaners, ribbon, blue jeans, etc.). Use a blue **bed** sheet for water in the **Building** and **Blocks** Center or as a parachute for Movement Time.

Boa Constrictor

Learn all about **boa constrictors**. Where do they live? What do they look like? What do they eat? Have the children draw pictures of boa constrictors.

Boat

Collect and show the children pictures of different types of **boats**. Talk about what each type of boat is used for and what type of water you might see the boat in (i.e., **barge** in the river, ship in the ocean, rowboat in a lake, canoe in stream). Play with toy boats in the water table or a **bathtub** at home.

Body Parts

Make a list of different **body parts**. Talk about what each body part is used for (eyes-see, legs-move around). Talk about the many different ways we can move our body parts (**blink**, **bend**, twist, stretch, squeeze). Then, encourage children to **bend** some of their body parts (knees, elbows, fingers, neck and waist).

Bolts

Purchase a variety of nuts and **bolts** from your local hardware store. Allow the children to explore how they fit together and come apart.

Bones

Learn about **bones**. How many bones does an average adult have? Why do we have bones? What do bones look like (skeleton)? Discuss if anyone has ever had or known someone who had a **broken** bone? What happened?

Boy
During attendance time, list all of the **boys** present and absent on a sheet of paper. Count the number of boys present and the number of boys absent.

Branch
Collect **branches** and allow the children to explore how they feel and look. Use the branches to write "B's" in the sand.

Brave
Read the story "**Brave** Bear" by Kathy Mallat, Scholastic Inc., 1999 or any other book about being brave. Talk about what makes someone **brave**. Allow the children to tell stories about a time when they knew someone who was acting brave.

Bread
Have a **bread** tasting party. Offer small pieces of some of the following types of breads: pumpernickel, rye, wheat, cinnamon raisin, pita, tortilla, **breadsticks, buns, bagels,** and taco shells. Have the children explore the bread with their senses. Taste, see, smell, touch, and even listen to the breads.

Breakfast/Bacon
Make **breakfast** menus to use in your Dramatic Play area. Using magazine/calendar pictures, create menus with typical breakfast items. Or collect breakfast menus from local restaurants to place in the center. Cook **bacon** for a **"breakfast"** snack. Children can use their senses to enjoy this special treat. See, smell and hear it cooking. Feel that it is warm and taste it.

Breathe
On a cold day, observe your own **breath**. Encourage children to take three deep, slow **breaths** to calm down when upset.

Breeze
Go outside on a **breezy** day. Talk about how it feels and what the breeze does to the plants and trees.

Bricks

If you have a **building** made from **brick**, then make **blue**, **black** or **brown brick** rubbings. Simply take sheets of tracing paper and fat crayons, without paper wrappers, and have the children hold or tape the paper on the brick wall and rub the side of the crayon on the paper. This will make an interesting brick impression. You can do the same thing with loose bricks in the classroom.

Bridge

Collect and show the children pictures of **bridges**. Talk about why we need bridges. Display the pictures in the **Blocks** and **Building** Center and encourage the children to construct bridges. Take photographs of their bridges and display them with the other pictures.

Brush

Place different types and sizes of **brushes** in a **bag** or **box**. Have the children take turns reaching into the bag, without looking, and describing what they feel. Talk about what the different types of brushes are used for. Ideas for different brushes: hair brush, paint brush, pastry brush, **bath/body** brush, nail brush and toothbrush.

Bubble

Blow **bubbles**. Add **blue** food coloring to the bubbles to make blue bubbles.

Bucket

Have a **bucket** partner race. Fill each team's bucket with the same amount of water. Place a stick horizontally through the handle of the bucket. One child holds one side of the handle the other holds the other side. They have to work together to get their bucket to the finish line without spilling the water. The team to the finish line with the most water is the winner. Measure the amount of water with a yardstick, if necessary.

Buffet

Go on a field trip to a local restaurant that serves food **buffet** style. Observe how the food is cooked and displayed. After the trip, create and serve your own "B" buffet. Serve some of the following items: **bagels**, **bread**, **bacon**, **brownie**, **banana (bread)**, **bologna**, **beef** sticks, **broccoli**, **boiled** eggs, **blackberries**, **blueberries** (muffins or pancakes) sprinkled with **brown** sugar, **brussel** sprouts, **bran** (cereal or muffins), **bread** or **butterscotch** pudding, three **bean** salad, **brown** rice, **buttermilk**, **biscuits**, and **beets**. Cut each item into **bite** sized servings and display them with word labels. The children can taste a little of each one that they choose. Send the list of "B" foods home for children to find "B" foods in their kitchen.

Bugs/Bees/Butterflies

Learn all about **bugs** (include **bees**, **butterflies** and **beetles**). **Buzz** like **bumblebees** on the way to the **bus**. Make coffee filter **butterflies**. Decorate the coffee filter with watered down paints using a dropper. Twist a colorful pipe cleaner around the center of the filter and form the ends into antennas. Look for more interesting ideas and information in the Early Childhood Thematic Book "Bees, Bugs, and Butterflies," Teacher's Friend Publications, 2001

Bugle

Invite an older student who can play the **bugle** to visit the classroom and demonstrate how it sounds, what it looks like, and how to play it.

Build/Building

Collect pictures of different types of **buildings** (different types of homes, apartment houses, grocery stores, fire house, library, post office, restaurant, etc.). Display the pictures in the **Blocks** and **Building** Center. Talk about the different types of structures and what they are used for. Encourage the children to use the different construction **blocks** and materials to build a variety of buildings. Take pictures of their buildings and display them along with the other pictures.

Bulb

Talk about plant **bulbs**, a large underground plant **bud**. Plant or show the children tulip bulbs. Watch the bulbs grow over time and **bloom** into flowers.

Bus

Invite a **bus** driver to your classroom to discuss bus safety rules with the children. Make a list of bus safety rules. Make Bus Safety **Badges** for the children to wear as a fun reward.

Butcher

Visit a local **butcher** in a butcher shop or the meat section of a grocery store. Learn about what butchers do, what types of equipment they use, what types of food they make, and how they display their food for sale to customers.

Butter

Make **butter** by shaking heavy cream in small jars. Add a little salt for taste and then serve the butter on **bagel** slices.

Button

Sort (by size, color, shape) and count colored **buttons** or enlarge the letter **"B"** and glue buttons on it. Lace **big** buttons on a string to make a necklace or **bracelet**. Use buttons in the Arts and Crafts Center to make colorful creations.

Other words that begin with the letter B:

These words may arise in naturally occurring conversations throughout the day/week. As you use these words, point out that they start with the letter "b" and write them on an index card to add to your word board.

basketball/baseball/bicycling (games/sports)

bathroom (room)

bench (a place to sit)

beneath/big/bottom (concepts)

black, blue, brown (colors)

break/broken (items getting broken or meaning the time when you leave one
        activity and then come back to it)

broom (clean-up time)

brother (family member)

buckle (buckling a belt after using the bathroom)

bump (bump on one's knee)

bunch (a bunch of flowers in a vase)

Bear
Pattern

Picture Cards

balloon

ball

boat

bicycle

bed

book

baby

butterfly

bird

TF1432 *Letter of the Week!*

Word Cards

bag	basket
bowl	ball
boat	belt
bark	boot
bandage	bell
book	bottle
bandana	bib
bus	bow

Trace and write the letters. Color the picture.

Name _____

Uppercase B

B B B B B B

Lowercase b

b b b b b b

My Alphabet Book

Name

I am learning about the letter B b. This is how I write it:

B B

b b

Here are some words that start with the letter B b:

This is my picture of a _____ .

Letter C

Name

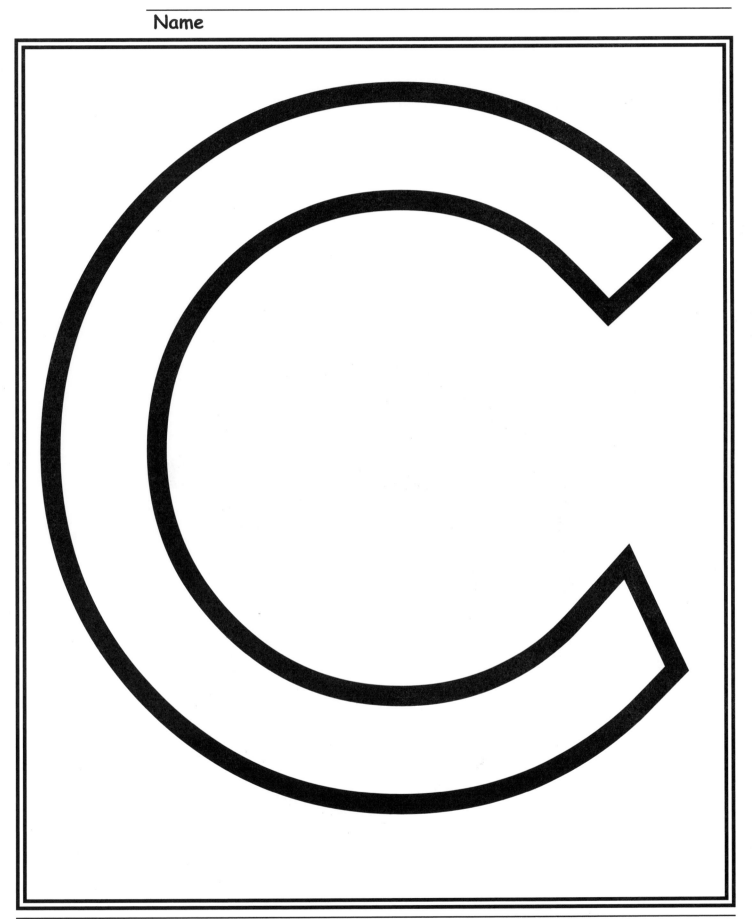

Letter c

Name

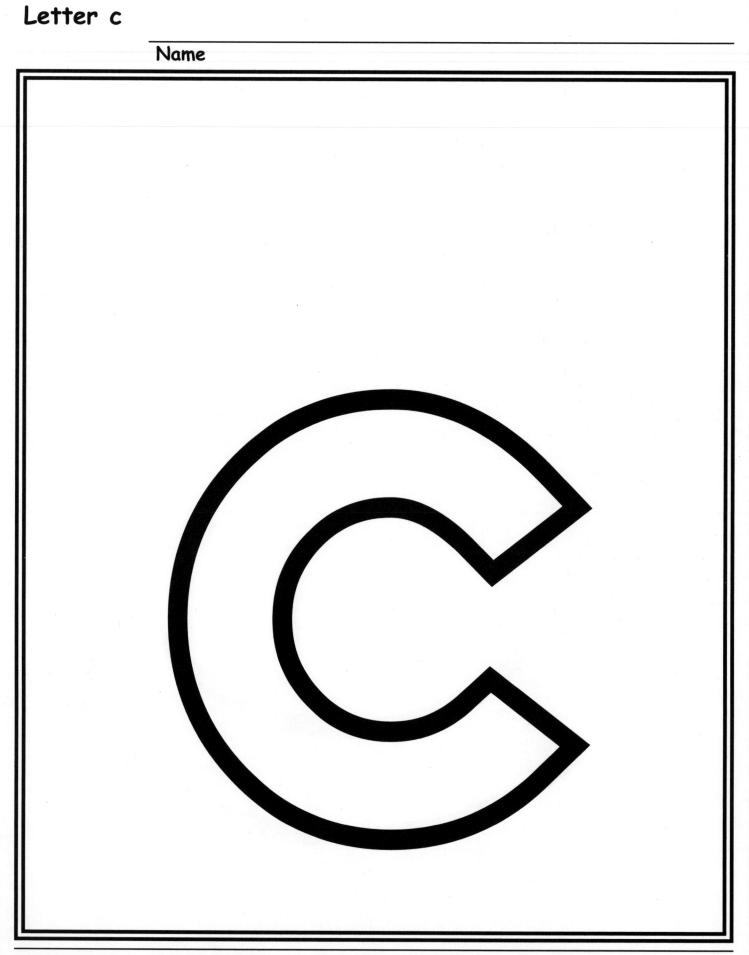

Ideas and Activities for the Letter:

Cafeteria
Visit the school **cafeteria**. Learn about: Who works in a cafeteria? What do they do each day? Who is the **chef/cook** or **cashier**? The chef or cook may be able to create a "**C**" menu for one day and demonstrate how foods are prepared.

Cake
Celebrate letter "**C**" week by making a **cake** shaped like a "**C**". Follow the directions on your favorite **chocolate** cake mix. After the cake is **cooked, cut** it in the shape of a "**C**". Frost the cake with **cream cheese** frosting.

Calendar
For one week or month, recall an event for each day. Keep a pictorial **calendar** by drawing a simple illustration depicting the event of the day.

Camel
Learn all about **camels**. A camel is a mammal with one or two humps on its back. It has large hoofs and is used in desert regions of Asia and Africa to transport people and products. Camels do not store water in the hump(s) on their backs. Rather, some members of the camel family store fat (food) in the hump(s).

Camera
Place **cameras** (old or toy) in the Dramatic Play **Center**. If you are able to, provide the **children** with an instant camera to take pictures. The children can instantly see the results of using a camera.

Candy Canes
Place the following "**C**" things in a box or at a table: **candy cane, cinnamon, cloves, coffee,** scented **candle,** and **cocoa.** They have different smells. Allow the children to smell the items.

Card
Demonstrate how to make a **card** by folding **construction** paper in half. Provide the materials to make a card in the Library/Writing **Center**. Praise the children who choose to make a card for being so **clever.**

Cardinal

Learn about birds that start with the letter "C", including **cranes, cardinals, chickens** and **crows**. Look for more interesting ideas and information in the Early Childhood Thematic Book "Feathered Friends," Teacher's Friend Publications, 2001.

Carnation

Demonstrate how **carnations** "drink" water through their stems. Place white carnations in a **clear** glass or vase. Add water. Add a few drops of food **coloring**. The carnation will gradually turn the **color**/shade of the dye in the food coloring.

Carnival/Circus

Attend a local **carnival** or **circus**. Or talk about what one might see at a carnival or circus. Make a list of the different things to "see," "eat," and "do" at one of these events. Look at and read books about the circus.

Carpenter

Tell the children that a **carpenter** is a person who builds or repairs wooden structures. Invite a carpenter to your classroom to demonstrate how they work, what tools they use, what type of safety equipment they use, and what type of products they produce. Play pretend carpenter in the Dramatic Play **Center** (include items such as tools, tool belt, gloves, goggles or safety glasses, wood scraps, glue).

Cartoon

Borrow books from your local library about how **cartoons** are made. Share the illustrations with the **children** so that they can see the process, step by step. Display the **comic** strips from the local paper on the bulletin board.

Caterpillar

Read the "Very Hungry **Caterpillar**" by Eric **Carle**. The **children** will learn how a caterpillar forms a **cocoon** and then changes into a beautiful butterfly. **Capture** and observe caterpillars in an empty aquarium in the Science **Center**.

Chain

Tell time with a link **chain**. Make a link type chain with strips of colored paper. Each link can represent one day. Count down the days before a special event, holiday, field trip or vacation by removing one link each day and counting the remaining links.

Chalk
Let the children **color** with sidewalk **chalk** outside.

Chopsticks
Show the children how to eat with **chopsticks** during snack time or lunch.

Chores
Make a list of **chores** that children can do. For example: set the table, make their bed, **clean** up their room, empty the dryer, fill the washing machine, fold towels, etc. Send the list home and ask the parents to have their child select one or two chores to complete each night/day. If the parents continue the activity over time, doing household chores will become part of their routine.

Circle
Fill a box with **circle** shaped items that start with the letter "C". Allow the children to discover that they are all circle shaped. Include some of the following items: **can, candle, clock, coffee can** with lid, **coins**, bottle **caps, coconut, cone, corks,** round **cake** pan, **checkers, cylinder**, and game **chips.**

City/Country
Teach about the name of the **city** and **country** that you live in. Show maps and puzzles of the United States.

Clam
Serve **clam chowder** for snack. Show the children a picture of a clam or provide clam shells to explore.

Clap
During attendance time, have each child **clap** the syllables in their full name.

Closet/Clothes
Have the children **clean** their **closets** as a home activity. Make a list of different types of **clothes** and other items found in their **closets**. Write the words on a sheet of paper.

Clouds

Lay on blankets or the grass and look up at the **clouds** while playing soft instrumental music during relaxation time. Talk to the children about the different shapes or forms that they see in the clouds. Enjoy their imaginations.

Clown

Talk about different types of **clowns** (in a **circus** or rodeo). What is their job? How do they make us laugh? Add clown **costumes**, trick bags/toys, and a mirror to the Dramatic Play **Center**.

Collect

Talk about the many different things that people **collect** (**coins**, stamps, rocks, special teacups, teddy bears, **cans/bottles**, etc.). Talk about why people collect different items. Invite family members and children to share their collections with the class. Or go outside into a grassy field and collect **clovers** or **colorful** stones.

Construction/Cranes

Play **construction** site in your Blocks and Building **Center**. Include these items: **cranes** and **construction** vehicles, trucks, tools, tool belts, wood scraps, maps, floor plans, blocks, **construction** signs, tape measure).

Cookies

Cook circle shaped **cookies**. Follow a recipe or package directions for your favorite circle shaped cookies. Cook them in an oven and serve for a special snack.

Corn

Eat **corn** on the **cob** for snack or paint with corn on the cob. Explore colorful, dry, Indian corn in the explore tub. Instruct the children to glue kernels of dried corn to create an interesting art project or roll small bits of tissue paper in the palms of their hands to make the corn kernels, and then glue in place.

Coupon

Clip grocery store **coupons** and sort them by food groups.

Cow/Calf

Learn about **cowboys** that herd **cattle (cows/calves)**. What do cowboys do everyday? What do the cows provide for people?

Crab

Use the **crab crawl** as a transition activity. For example, as the children move from circle to wash their hands before snack time, have them take turns crawling like crabs to the sink.

Cross

Practice writing **crosses** with **crayons** in the Library/Writing **Center**.

Cry

Talk about things that make us feel sad or **cry**. Children should know that it is ok to cry when they are hurt or sad. They should learn about who can help them when they feel sad.

Cube

Have a "cube" day. Stack, sort, or **count colored cubes** in the Math and Manipulatives Center. Play a cube game during movement time. (Ideas can be found in the Teacher's Friend Early Childhood Thematic Books.) Cube snack: offer the following foods **cut** into **cubes** (demonstrate how to cut them into cubes): **cheddar cheese, cantaloupe, carrots** and **cucumbers**. Serve the cubed foods in **cups**. Serve ice **cubes** in their juice.

Curly

Count how many **children** in the **class** have **curly** hair. Invite the children with curly hair to line up first or sit down first.

Cut

Cut clay snakes with scissors in the Arts and **Crafts Center**. Provide paper and scissors and allow the children to snip and cut at their own pace. Easy patterns can be found in the book "Little Kids Can...Cut," Teacher's Friend Publications, 2000.

caterpillar

Other words that begin with the letter C:

These words may arise in naturally occurring conversations throughout the day/week. As you use these words, point out that they start with the letter "c" and write them on an index card to add to your word board.

cat (child's pet)

cab, caboose, canoe, car (vehicles)

caps, capes (dramatic play)

carpet (on floor)

carton (of milk)

catch (a ball)

cauliflower, or **cherries** (food)

chain (on fence)

chairs (furniture in a classroom)

cheek or chin (body parts)

Christmas (holiday)

climb (outside)

comb (hair)

computer (equipment)

cousin (a child's relative)

cat

cloud

Picture Cards

crab

cactus

cake

calendar

car

caterpillar

cone

cup

corn

 TF1432 Letter of the Week!

Word Cards

can	car
cork	cookie cutter
cookbook	cactus
calendar	card
coat	cradle
candle	cup
coin	cow
corn	comb

Trace and Write

Trace and write the letters. Color the picture.

Name

Uppercase C

C C C C C C C

Lowercase c

c c c c c c c

My Alphabet Book

Name

I am learning about the letter C c.
This is how I write it:

Here are some words that start with the letter C c:

This is my picture of a _____.

Letter D

Name

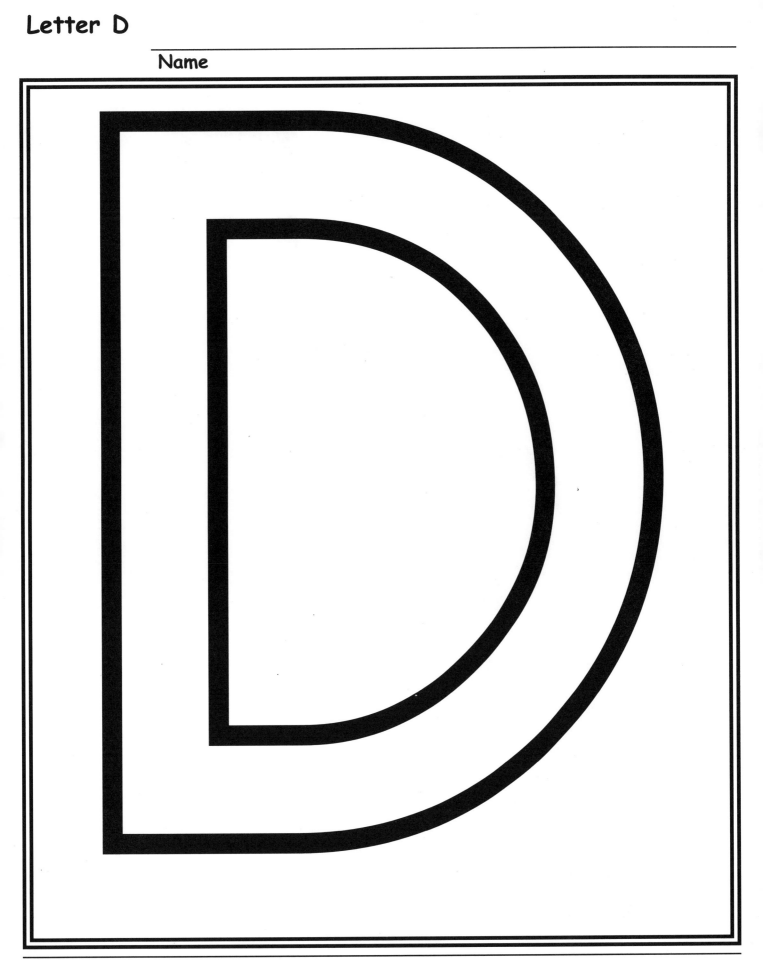

Letter d

Name

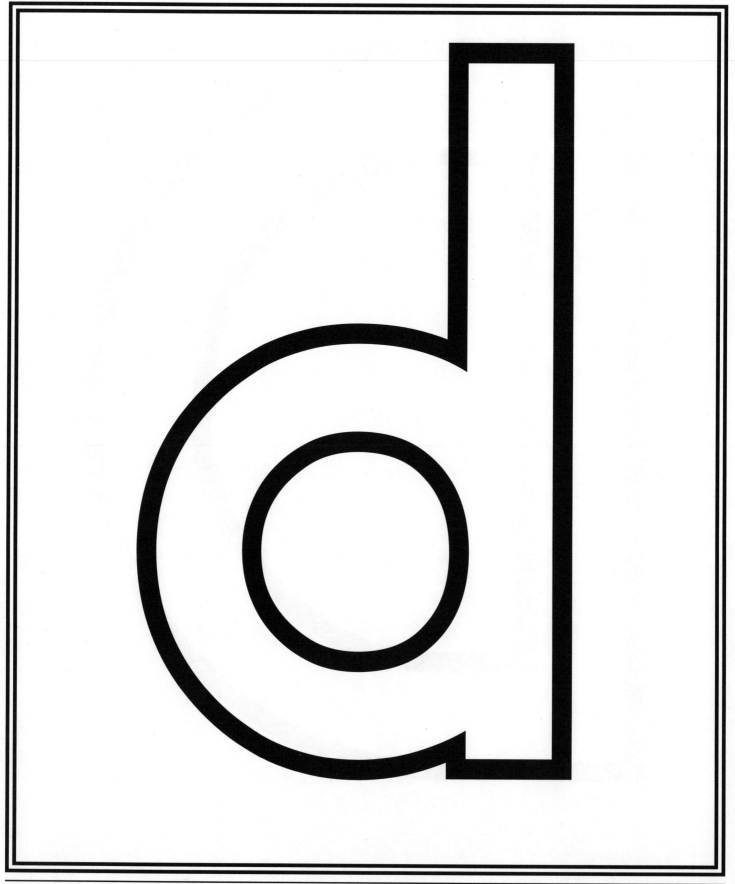

Ideas and Activities for the Letter:

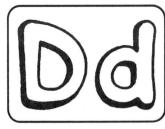

Dad
Write a **Dear Dad** letter. Encourage the children to tell Dad how much they love him.

Dance
Dance to music from **Disney's** 101 **Dalmatians** soundtrack.

Deck of Cards
Collect various old or incomplete **decks** of cards. Have the children sort through the cards and separate all the "1's", "2's", etc. Or remove all of the aces and face cards and have the children take turns selecting two cards and adding them together on paper for mathematics.

Degrees
Record the temperature in **degrees** for 20 school **days** on a chart. Is it getting warmer or colder?

Delivery Van
Make a **Delivery** Van **Driver** Badge. Have the children take turns wearing the badge as they deliver letters/notes or packages to other classrooms or the office.

Dentist
Learn about **dentists** and how they help people. Look for interesting information on the following websites:
www.toothfairy.org   www.mypediatricdentist.com   kids-world.colgatepalmolive.com

Dialing
Instruct the children to practice **dialing** their phone numbers on an old telephone.

Diamond
Practice tracing and **drawing diamonds**. Instruct the children to make simple diamonds by drawing a "V" on the bottom and a "V" on the top.

Dice

Instruct the children to roll two large toy **dice** and add or subtract the numbers on paper for mathematics.

Dictionary

Add children's **dictionaries** to the Library/Writing Center. Make a dictionary with the picture cards throughout this book. Copy and cut out several of the pictures for each letter. Purchase a large pad of white paper for each student. The pad must have at least 26 pages in it. At the top of each page write each letter in alphabetical order (one letter per page). Through out the year the children can glue the picture cards to the correct pages and at the end of the year they will each have their own picture dictionary.

Different

Discuss the various things that make each one of us **different** from one another. Make a written list on a large sheet of paper. Examples might be: size of one's family, parents, the home one lives in, address, phone number, color of eyes/hair, height, weight, sports that one can do, things one might be good at or like to do, clothes, etc.

Dinosaurs

Learn all about **dinosaurs**. Talk about each dinosaur's different features (tails, necks, wings, heads, spikes, etc.) Hide plastic dinosaurs in the sand and have the children pretend to be archeologists. Sort and count dinosaurs by type.

Dirt

Hide **dimes** in the **dirt** or sand table and have the children **dig** them up.

Doctor

Pretend to be **doctors** in the **Dramatic** Play Center. Include items such as doctor kits, white shirts or smocks, uniforms or hats, play doctor's equipment, cot or mat, strips of torn white sheets (bandages), empty bandage boxes, face masks, gloves, and cotton balls).

Dogs

Learn about **dogs** that help people (i.e., seeing eye dogs, hearing ear dogs, guard/police dogs, and fire dogs). Invite a trainer/owner of one of these special dogs to your school. What special skills do they have to learn? Who trains them for their jobs? How do they help people?

Dolls

Practice individual **dressing** skills by dressing up **dolls**. Include **diapers** for the baby dolls. Wash the dolls in the water table.

Dollar

Sort coins to add up to a **dollar**. How many different combinations are there? How many **dimes** equal one dollar?

Dozen

Teach the children that a **dozen** equals twelve of something. Eggs usually come in a dozen. What else comes in a dozen? (**donuts,** rolls, muffins, bagels, etc.) Count a dozen blocks, small cars, beads, pieces of cereal, etc. Use an egg carton or muffin tray to help the children sort or count to twelve.

Dragon

Help the children **draw dragons**. Provide paper and crayons or markers. Give the following verbal **directions** to the children. "We are going to draw dragons today. Draw a large purple body with **dots** and four legs. Give your dragon a big mouth. Draw a long green tail and two large eyes. Draw zig-zag or triangle spikes on its back. Give your dragon a name and write the name below your dragon on your paper."

Drum

Let the children play the **drums**. Use commercially produced drums or make drums from oatmeal containers or coffee cans.

Other words that begin with the letter D:

These words may arise in naturally occurring conversations throughout the day/week. As you use these words, point out that they start with the letter "d" and write them on an index card to add to your word board.

daffodil, daisy, dandelion (flowers)
denim (jeans)
desk (furniture in a classroom)
desert (place)
dish (something one puts food on)
dolphin (animal)
dominos (game)
doodle (on paper)

door (classroom entrance/exit)
down (opposite of up)
drill (toy in Blocks and Building Center)
drink, dessert (at snack or lunch time)
dry (paintings dry on a rack)
duck (bird)
dusting/dirty (clean-up time)

Picture Cards

dolphin

dinosaur

dice

dollar

doll

desk

door

duck

dog

Word Cards

diaper	dice
dictionary	dominos
doll	dinosaur
dish	denim
dowel	duck
dime	doctor kit
dough	deck of cards
dolphin	dandelion

Trace and Write

Trace and write the letters. Color the picture.

Name

Uppercase D

D D D D D D D D

Lowercase d

d d d d d d

My Alphabet Book

Name _____

I am learning about the letter D d.
This is how I write it:

D D

d d

Here are some words that start with the letter D d:

_____   _____

_____   _____

_____   _____

This is my picture of a _____.

Letter E

Name

Letter e

Name

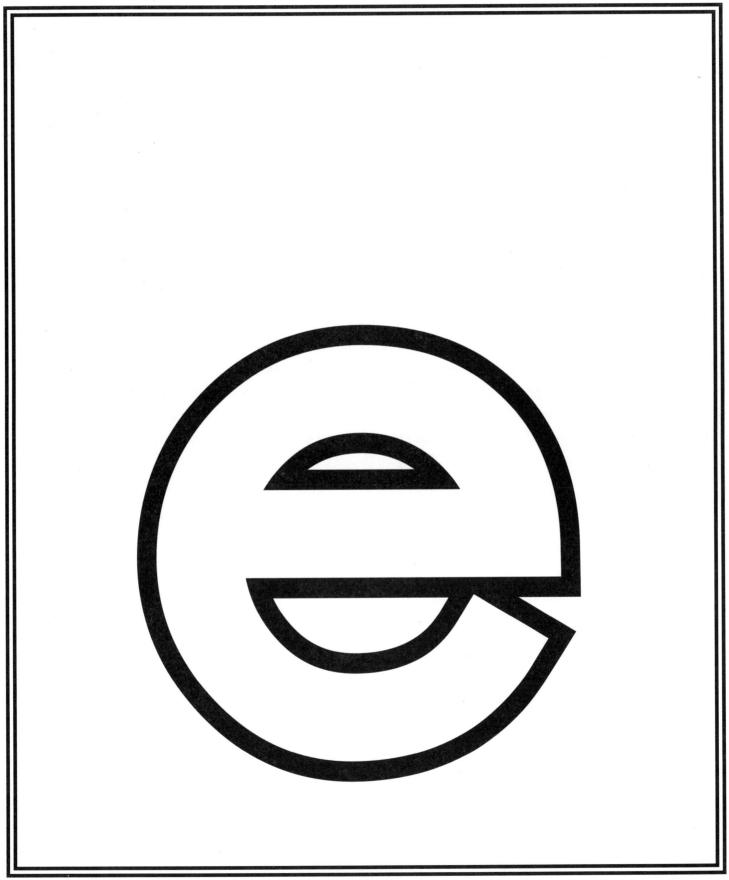

Ideas and Activities for the Letter:

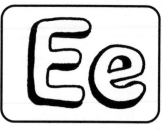

Ears/Eyes

Learn about the senses of hearing **(ears)** and sight **(eyes)**.

The sense of hearing occurs through the ear, its structures and the brain.

Probably the most important thing that we hear are words that can be spoken, whispered, shouted or sung. People who cannot hear or hear well are known to be deaf or have a hearing impairment. They may wear hearing aids (tiny microphones in their ears). These people often have trouble speaking, as well. They use sign language, read lips, and/or use Hearing Ear Dogs to help them have productive lives.

The sense of sight provides us with information such as color, depth, size, texture, and shape of objects. It also lets us know about lightness and darkness. People who cannot see or have difficulty seeing are known to be blind or have a visual impairment. These people often walk with a white cane or use the services of a Seeing Eye Dog.

The following eye and ear equipment and safety items can be added to the Dramatic Play Center: eye chart, protective face masks (something an athlete might wear), face shields (something a welder might wear), safety goggles or glasses, eye muffs or plastic ear protectors, hard hats, binoculars, magnifying glasses, sunglasses, child's telescope, child's microscope, child's microphone, and headphones. More ideas and information can be found in the Early Childhood Thematic Book "Nose to Toes," Teacher's Friend Publications, 2001.

Earth

Explain that the planet we live on is called the **Earth.** Show the children a picture of the Earth or a globe. It is made of water, land, and sky. Discuss ways to keep our Earth clean and safe. Discuss and model how to conserve and recycle our natural resources.

Eat

Serve "E" foods for snack or lunch, such as scrambled **eggs, egg** drop soup, **eggnog, enchiladas, eggplant, egg** rolls, or **English** muffins.

Eggs

Make and **eat** hard-boiled **eggs.** Use the **eggshells** in the Arts and Crafts Center.

Eight/Eleven
Count out **eight** or **eleven** blocks, cars, trucks, crayons, etc.

Elephants
Learn about **elephants**. There are two types of elephants. African elephants have large ears and Asiatic or Indian elephants have smaller ears. Elephants have trunks that are approximately 5 feet in length and are used for breathing, smelling, gathering food and water, cooling off, and communicating with other elephants. An elephant's trunk can hold more than 2 gallons of water at one time. Many elephants stand about 11 ft. tall and 24 ft. long and weigh approximately 14,000 lbs. They have large ears (which they flap to keep cool), gray wrinkly skin, swishy tails, and large stump-like legs. They eat leaves, grass, small branches, bark, coconuts, and berries. They live for 50 to 70 years.

Emotions
Talk about our **emotions**. What are emotions? How do they make us look and feel? Make a wheel using the words sad, happy, angry and afraid. Let the children spin the arrow on the wheel and act out the emotion shown.

Empty
Collect **empty egg** cartons. Add them to the Arts and Crafts Center. See how many different things the children can make from them.

End
Read a story **each** day. At the **end** of each story discuss the **endings**. Ask the children to make up different endings to the stories.

Envelope/Eraser
Add **envelopes** and **erasers** to the Library/Writing Center for use by the children.

Eskimos
Learn about **Eskimos**. Where do they live? What types of homes do they live in? How do they get from one place to another?

Exercise
Purchase or rent a child's **exercise** tape or make up your own exercise routine and do the exercises with the children. Always watch videotapes before showing them to the children to ensure that they are appropriate for the age group and ability level. Children should be provided with the opportunity to exercise their muscles on a daily basis. Include a movement or outside play time each day in your lesson plans.

Exit/Entrance

Take a walk throughout the school and locate and count all of the **exit/entrance** signs. Does every outside door have an exit sign?

Experiment

Conduct a simple **experiment** to see what types of objects float and which objects sink. Make a chart with the heading "Float or Sink Experiment" depicting their discoveries. Some items to experiment with: stones, corks, pencils, cotton balls, plastic cups, paperclips, apples, pennies

Other words that begin with the letter E:

These words may arise in naturally occurring conversations throughout the day/week. As you use these words, point out that they start with the letter "e" and write them on an index card to add to your word board.

early (time of day)

Easter (holiday)

elbow (body part)

end (person at back of the line)

equal (math/science)

extraordinary/excellent (use these words when praising children's behavior/work)

elephant

Picture Cards

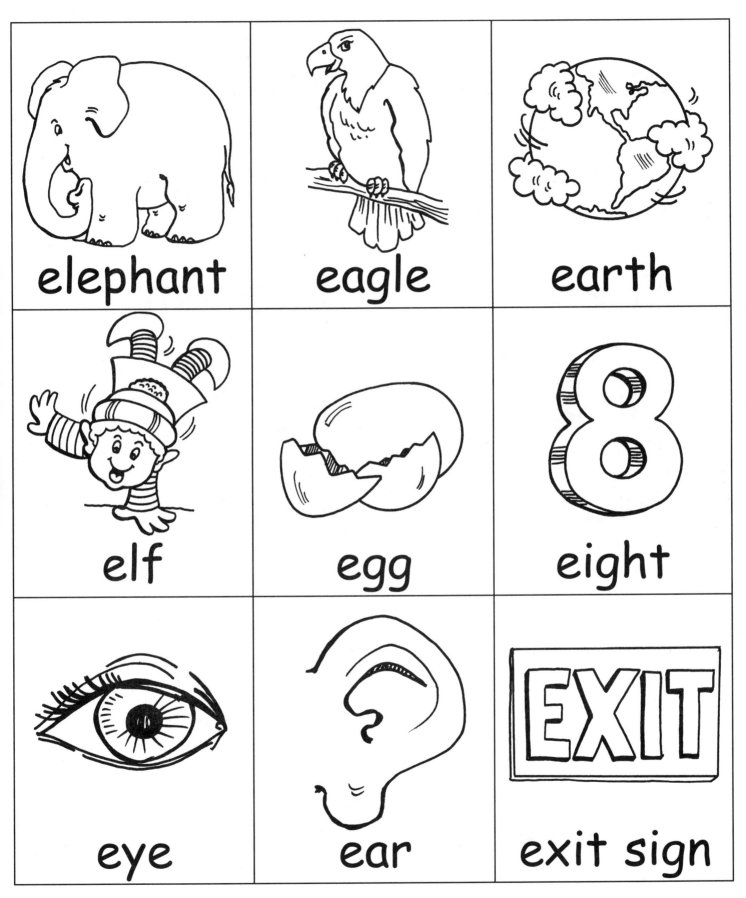

elephant

eagle

earth

elf

egg

eight

eye

ear

exit sign

TF1432 Letter of the Week!

Word Cards

ear muffs	eggs
egg carton	eye chart
eraser	elephant
engine	eight
evergreen	earth
envelope	elf
exit sign	eggplant
entrance sign	eleven

Trace and Write

Trace and write the letters. Color the picture.

Name _____

Uppercase E

Lowercase e

Name

I am learning about the letter E e.
This is how I write it:

Here are some words that start with the letter E e:

This is my picture of an _____ .

Letter F

Name

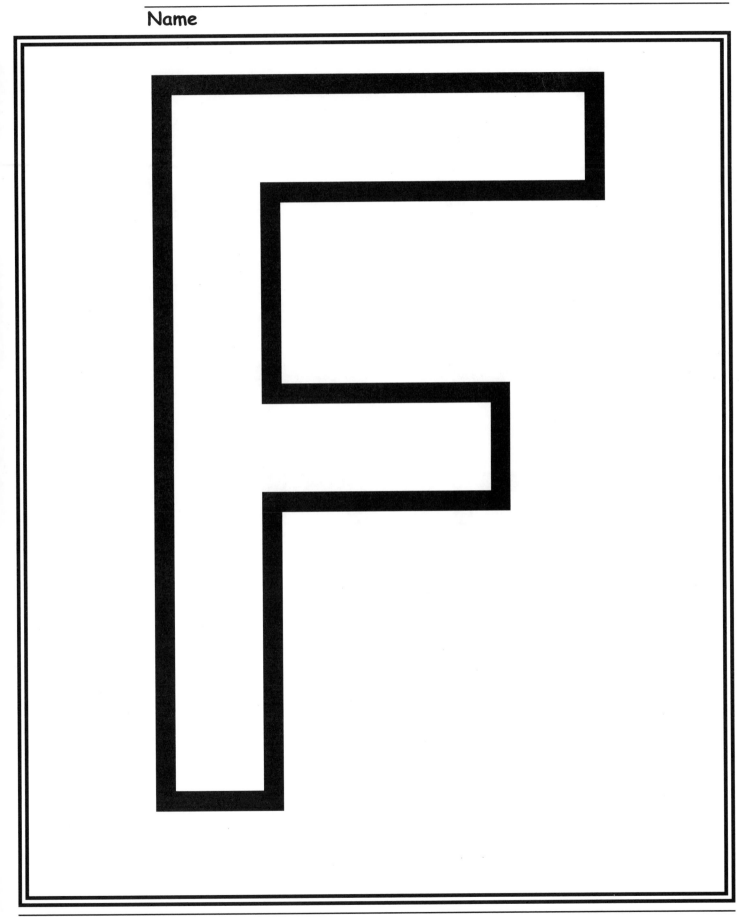

Name

Ideas and Activities for the Letter:

Fabric
Provide a variety of different **fabric** scraps (including **felt** and **fur**). Instruct the children to make a fabric collage by gluing the fabrics to squares of poster board. While the children explore the fabrics, encourage them to describe the different colors, patterns, and textures.

Face
Make **funny faces** in a mirror. Talk about the ways that we can move the different parts of our face (eyes, nose, mouth, cheeks, forehead).

Family
Invite the children to share **family** photos with their classmates. Talk about the different members of each child's family. Display the photos on a bulletin board or in a photo album.

Fan
Have the children make simple **fans**. **Feathers** can be glued to the fan. Have the children fan themselves and **feel** the air blowing.

Farm
Name things found on a **farm**. Discuss what each item or animal is used for on a farm. Look for other interesting ideas and information in the Early Childhood Thematic Book, "Farm Animals," Teacher's Friend Publications, 2001.

Feet
Paint with your **feet**. This can be messy. If you can, complete this activity outdoors. Roll out a long sheet of white bulletin board paper. At one end, place a tray of paint and at the other end a bucket of water and towels. An adult can paint the bottom of the child's feet with a brush, then the child walks across the paper. Have another adult help each child wash off the paint. Display the **foot-print** mural on the class board.

Fire
Learn about **fire** safety rules. Check with your local fire station for resources. Talk about the different ways that fire can be helpful (to cook/warm food, to heat homes, candles for birthdays, fireworks, for light, etc.) You can also list ways that fire can be harmful (destroy people and property, burn forests, destroy animal homes, hurt/burn people).

Fish

Make a **fish** pattern and have the children cut out the fish and then draw on the **fins** and gills.

Flag

Show the children the American **flag** and your state flag. Talk about the different colors, shapes, and symbols.

Flashlight

Play with **flashlights** in a dimly lit or dark room.

Float

Make simple boats from craft sticks and plastic or Styrene foam bowls or containers. Attach the sticks with a small amount of clay. **Float** the boats in the water table or bathtub.

Flower

Pick, smell or plant **flowers**. Draw or paint flowers. Paint with dandelions.

Fly

Help the children **fly** a kite or make a paper airplane. Make a list of different things that fly.

Fold

Practice **folding** colored paper or paper napkins at lunch time.

Forest

Make a list of animals and things **found** in a **forest**.

Freckles

Instruct the children with **freckles** to line up **first** on your way to lunch.

Freeze

Freeze water and observe it turning into ice.

Frighten

Talk about things that **frighten** us or make us **fearful**. Discuss things that the children can do when they are frightened.

Frog

Make a **Fabulous Friendly Frog** Award. Give these awards to children that are demonstrating acts of **friendship** or kindness.

Funnel

Play with **funnels** in a tub of water or sand.

Other words that begin with the letter F:

These words may arise in naturally occurring conversations throughout the day/week. As you use these words, point out that they start with the letter "f" and write them on an index card to add to your word board.

fat, few, first, full (concepts)

father, friend (people)

February (month)

finish (completing an activity)

fist, forehead, finger (body parts)

five, four (numbers)

floor (part of room)

fork, food, fruit, French toast (meal time)

Friday (day of the week)

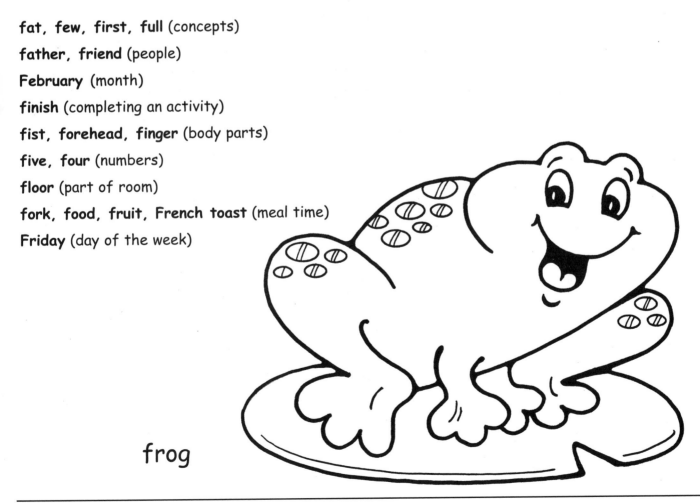

frog

Picture Cards

fan

feet

fox

finger

five

feather

fish

fire

fork

Word Cards

farm	fan
feather	fork
fish	foil
five	four
funnel	fabric
first aid kit	felt
flashlight	flag
frame	frog

Trace and Write

Trace and write the letters. Color the picture.

Name _____

Uppercase F

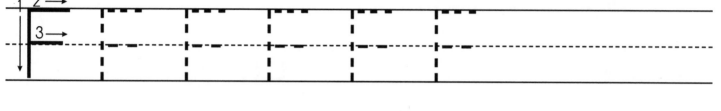

Lowercase f

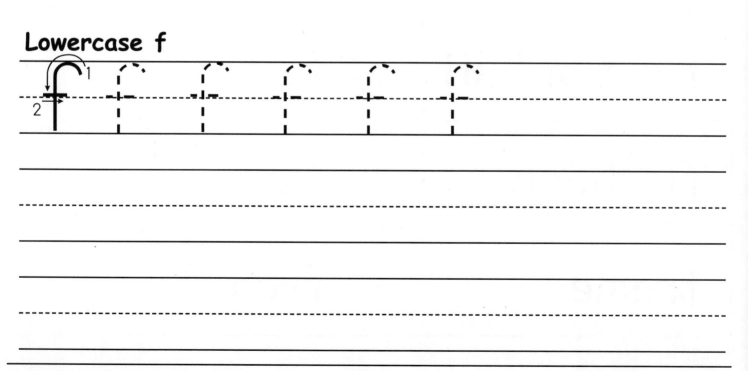

My Alphabet Book

_____

Name

I am learning about the letter F f.
This is how I write it:

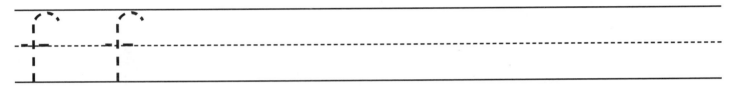

Here are some words that start with the letter F f:

This is my picture of a _____ .

Letter G

Name _____

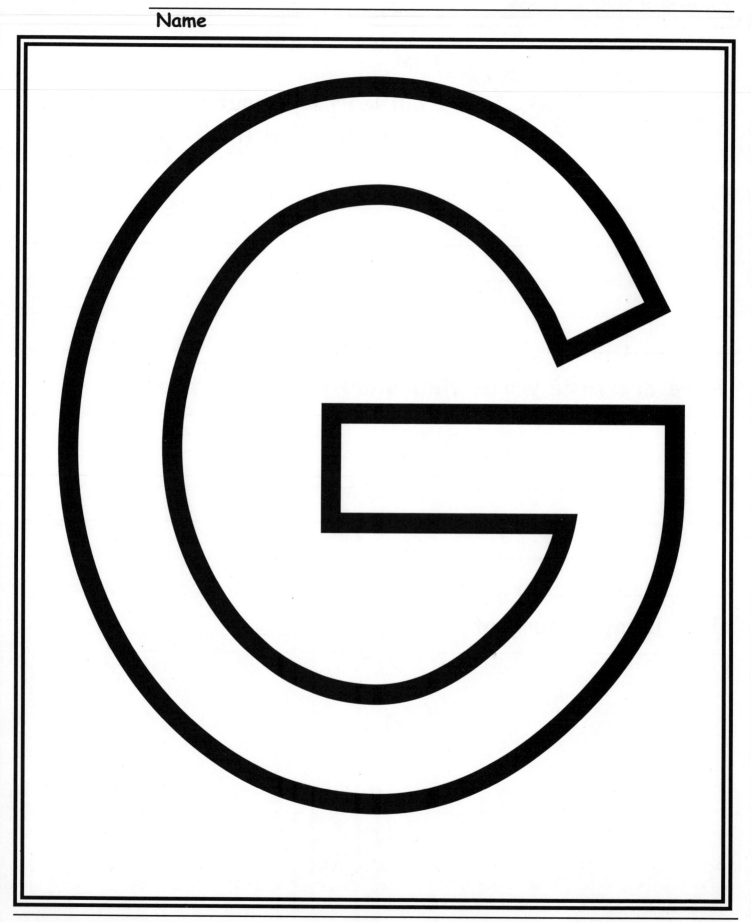

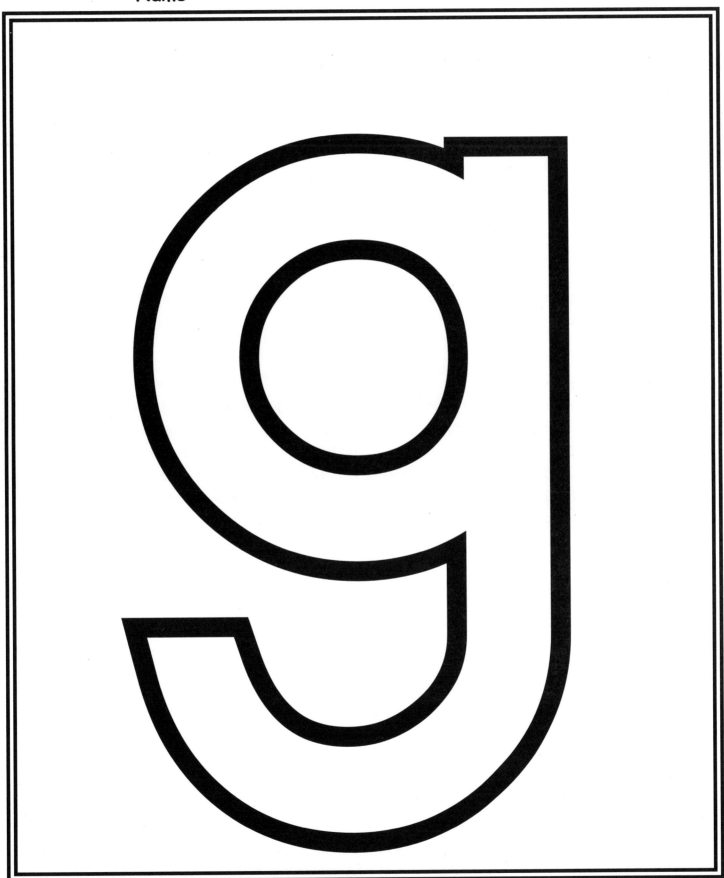

Ideas and Activities for the Letter:

Gallon
Use a scale or balance to weigh and measure a **gallon** of different liquids.

Gallop
Play a relay **game**. Separate the class into two or three teams. Each team's members take turns **galloping** to a basket filled with **gloves.** They find a matching pair of gloves and gallop back to their team and the next person takes a turn. The game ends with the first team who has every member holding or wearing a matching pair of gloves.

Garbage
Clean up the **garbage** in the neighborhood, play yard or a nearby park. If possible, watch the garbage trucks collect the school's garbage.

Garden/Greenhouse/Grass
Read stories about all the different things that **grow** in a **garden**. Plant a small school garden or build a **greenhouse**. Talk about the tools used in gardening. Add toy garden tools and garden **gloves** to the outside sandbox. Harvest some of the vegetables and make a garden salad and serve them with salad dressing or dip. Visit a local greenhouse and learn about how a greenhouse works. **Grow grass** in a clear plastic cup. Fill small clear cups with soil and sprinkle on grass seeds. Water and observe the roots and grass grow. The children can watch the grass grow. They can then cut the grass with kid-safe scissors.

Gift
Make a **gift** for someone special. Provide wrapping paper, bows and tape.

Giggle
Encourage the children to tell riddles then have fun watching the children **giggle**.

Giraffe
Learn about **giraffes**. Giraffes are the tallest of all animals, up to 18 ft. tall and weighing over 4,000 lbs. They have short upstanding manes, the same number of neck bones as all other animals, sharp eyesight, and unique pattern of patches (like human fingerprints). They eat leaves from acacia trees and twigs from tops of trees. They live in Africa and travel in "herds."

Girl
Invite all of the **girls** wearing something **green** to line up first.

Glasses
Encourage the children to wear funny **glasses** (clown glasses, sunglasses, glasses with spring eyes, **goggles**, etc.) in the Dramatic Play Center.

Globe
Look at a **globe** to find where you live and other places of interest.

Gold/Gray/Green
Use **gold/gray/green** paint with brushes at the easels. Play "I See Something **Green**." Eat green foods for snack (**grapes**, cucumbers, peas, string beans, mint ice cream, pickles, green Jello®.) Make a nature collage with green items (**grass**, leaves, buds, needles, moss, clovers). Invite the children to either wear something green or bring something green to school. Encourage them to talk about what they wore or brought to Show and Tell. Dance with green ribbons.

Golf
Use a hammer to pound **golf** tees into blocks of Styrofoam. Have the children play golf with a child's golf set.

Grandparents
Write a note to a **grandparent**. Invite **grandparents** to be special **guests** for a snack of **grapes**, **grapefruit**, **granola**, **graham crackers**, and **grape** or **grapefruit** juice.

Grasshopper
Collect **grasshoppers** and keep them in a clear tank with a net cover. Allow the children to observe and listen to them.

Grate
Grate cheese for macaroni and cheese or tacos or cheese wraps (sprinkle cheese over a tortilla and warm up in an oven until the cheese melts. Roll them into wraps).

Groceries

Make a list of things found in a **grocery** store. Ask the children to help their parents unpack the **groceries** and put them away.

Grow

Write a list of things that **grow** (children, plants, flowers, trees, **grass**, weeds, hair, fingernails, animals). Plant flowers or a tree in the schoolyard. Observe the **growing** changes over the school year.

Grownup

Ask: "What is a **grownup**?", "What can grownups do that you wish you could do?" or "What do you think you might like to do when you are a grownup?" Write their responses on a large sheet of paper.

Guitar

Listen to a tape of **guitar** music. Ask a local musician to come to your class and play the guitar.

Other words that begin with the letter G:

These words may arise in naturally occurring conversations throughout the day/week. As you use these words, point out that they start with the letter "g" and write them on an index card to add to your word board.

garages (Building and Blocks Center)

gate (outside)

glad, good, gentle (interactions)

glue (art)

go, give (directions)

goodbye, good morning, good night (greetings)

graph (math/science)

grill (cooking)

gum (candy)

gym (place in a school)

gift

Picture Cards

game

gate

gift

giraffe

girl

goose

gum

goat

guitar

Word Cards

globe	gloves
goggles	gourd
guitar	greenhouse
garlic	game
griddle	giraffe
glasses	golf ball
grass	grate
garbage can	garage

Trace and Write

Trace and write the letters. Color the picture.

Name

Uppercase G

G G G G G G

Lowercase g

g g g g g g

My Alphabet Book

Name

I am learning about the letter G g. This is how I write it:

Here are some words that start with the letter G g:

This is my picture of a _____.

Name

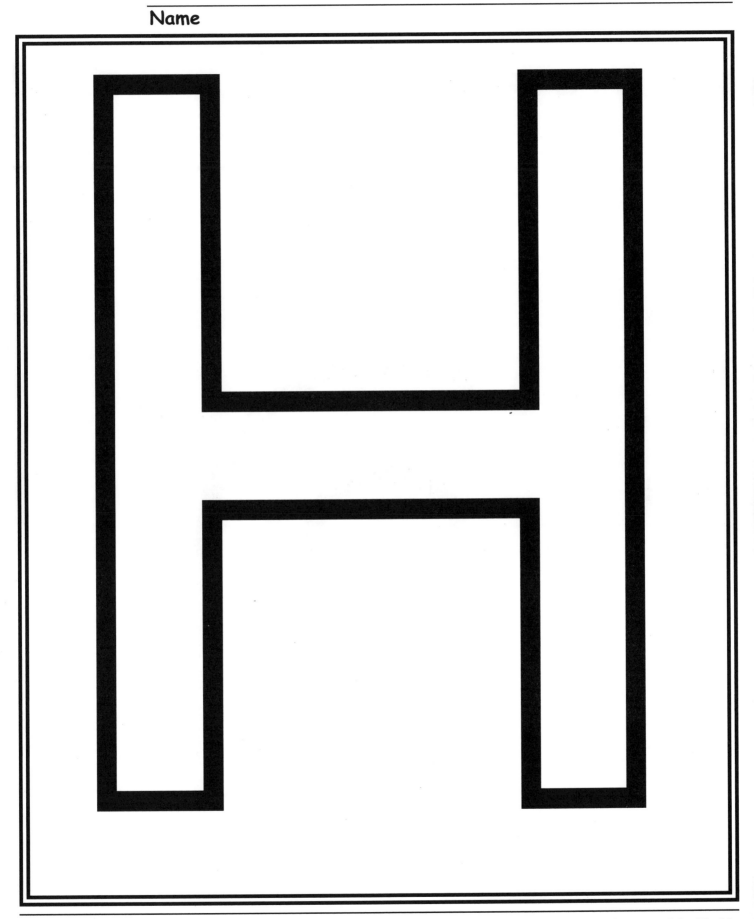

Letter h

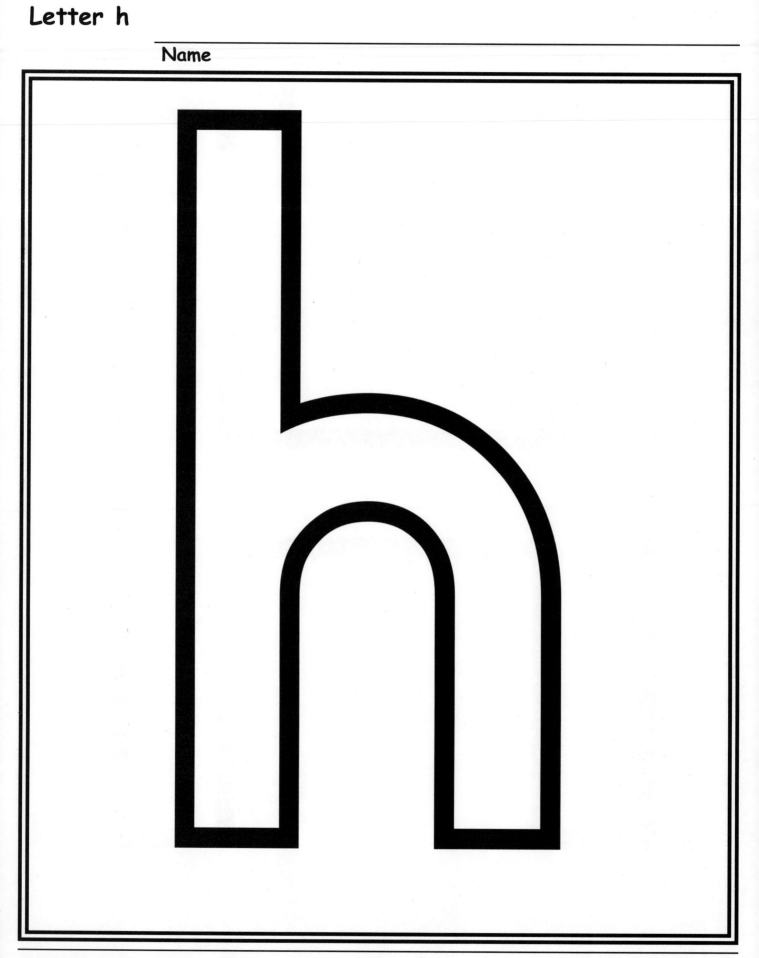

Ideas and Activities for the Letter:

Hair
Talk about color of **hair**. Make a hair color chart using the children in your classroom. Have the children count the number of children that have red hair, brown hair, etc. Make up simple math problems by having the children add up the number of children with brown hair and the number of children with blonde hair.

Half
Have a "**half**" day. Cut **hamburgers** and **hotdogs** in half. (Do this in front of the children.) Fill cups half full of **hot** chocolate. Cut straws or construction paper shapes in half. Read the first half of a story and ask the children to make up the second half.

Hamster
Keep a pet **hamster** for your classroom. Teach the children about hamsters, what they eat, what they do all day, and how to care for them.

Hands
Make a list of things to do with your **hands**. Examples might be to clap, rub your stomach, pick up a fork, scratch an itch, wiggle fingers, write with a pencil, shake hands, etc.

Hard
Pass around a wooden block during Circle Time. Ask the children to describe how it feels (smooth, **hard**). Then ask them to name other things that feel hard.

Hat
Play "Whose **Hat** Is It?" Fill a bag with a variety of hats, such as fire fighter, police officer, chef, nurse, doctor, clown, baseball, etc. Children can take turns pulling a hat out, trying it on and telling about who might wear it and why.

Head
Encourage each child to draw a picture of **his** or **her head**. Note the various face parts and ask the children to include them in their pictures. Try this activity at the beginning of the school year and then again at the end. Notice the changes in the details of their drawings.

Heart

Cut **hearts** from construction paper. Cover the heart patterns with small pieces of paper or tissue paper. Encourage the children to pinch and tear the paper or roll the tissue paper in the palms of their hands and then glue the pieces in place.

Height

Measure and record each child's **height**.

Hello

Learn how to say "**Hello**" in different languages. Spanish (**Hola**), French (Bonjour), Chinese (Nei ho), **Hebrew** (Shalom), and Japanese (Konichiwa)

Herb

Gather several **herbs**. Label the herbs and allow the children to explore and smell them. Good examples are basil, rosemary, dill, lemon grass, chives, mint, etc.

Hero

Name the characteristics that make someone a **hero**. Make a list of people that the children believe are **heroes**.

Hibernate

Learn about animals that **hibernate** (those animals who spend the winter in a restful or sleeping state).

Hole

Have the children name things that have a **hole** in them. Examples might be a bagel, inner tube, donut, tire, straw, ring, CD, ear, etc.

Holiday

Make a list of **holidays**. Ask the children to list their favorite holidays.

Home

Write a list of things found in a **home**. Ask the children the difference between a **house** and a home.

Hoop/Hop

Line up several **hoola hoops**. Instruct the children to **hop** through the hoops. See who can hop on one foot or hop in place the longest.

Horn
Blow or **honk** party **horns.**

Hospital
Learn about different places that begin with the letter "H," such as **hotel, hospital, home/house, harbor.** Who works and/or lives in these places? What kinds of things **happen** in each place?

Hot
List things that might feel **hot.** Talk about reasons not to touch hot things. Talk about the benefits of some hot things. For example: campfires provide **heat** for warmth and light so that one can see; hot water is used to clean and kill germs.

Hundred
Count one **hundred** pennies, buttons or paperclips.

Other words that begin with the letter H:
These words may arise in naturally occurring conversations throughout the day/week. As you use these words, point out that they start with the letter "h" and write them on an index card to add to your word board.

Halloween, Hanukkah (holiday)

hammer (building)

heavy, high (concepts)

heel, hip (body parts)

helicopter (vehicle)

hockey (game)

hood, hanger, hook (during arrival/departure time)

horse (animal)

hose, hydrant (found outside)

hour (time)

hug, happy, honest (emotions)

hungry (snack/lunch)

hurricane (weather)

hurt, help (accident)

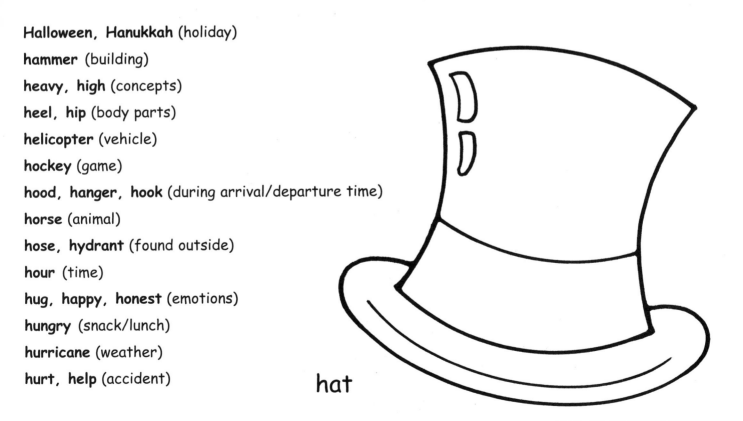

hat

Picture Cards

heart

hammer

hamburger

hen

hand

house

hose

horn

hat

Word Cards

hammer	hamster
handkerchief	hay
hook	heart
hoop	horn
hammock	helicopter
herb garden	hamper
hanger	hat
hockey stick	hoe

Trace and Write

Trace and write the letters. Color the picture.

Name

Uppercase H

Lowercase h

My Alphabet Book

Name

I am learning about the letter H h.
This is how I write it:

Here are some words that start with the letter H h:

This is my picture of a _____.

Letter I

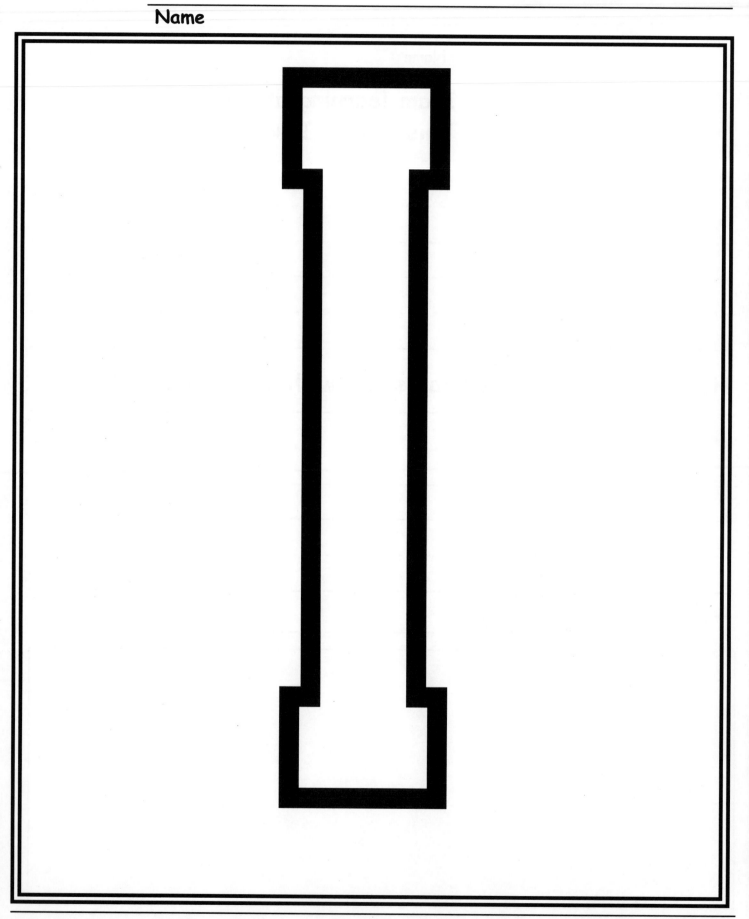

Letter i

Name

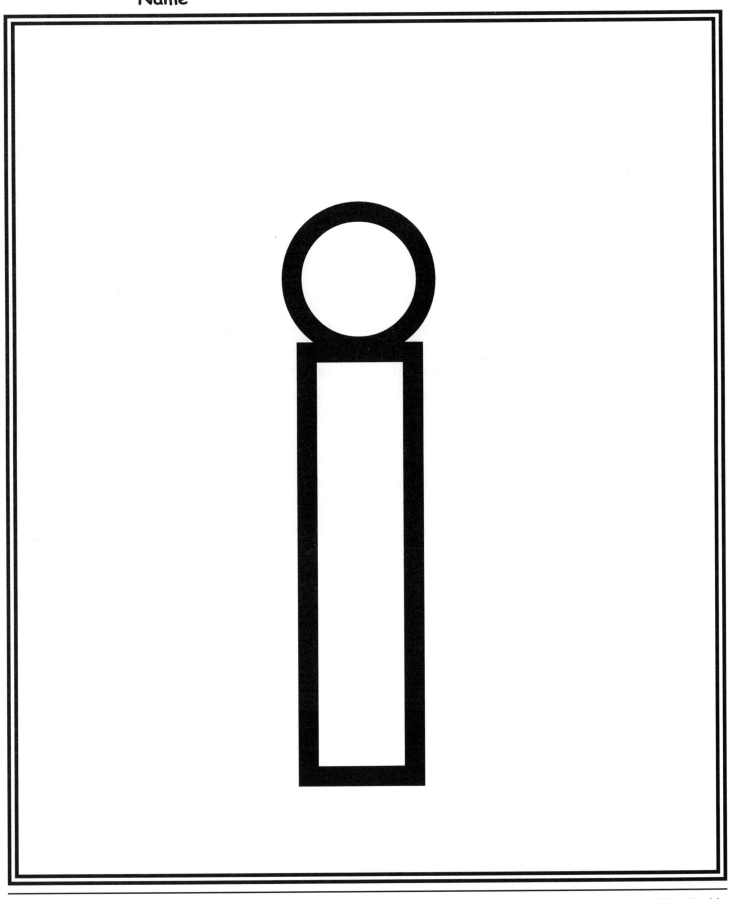

95

Ideas and Activities for the Letter:

Ice

Observe how **ice** turns into water. Fill a jug with ice cubes and, over the day, watch how it melts into water. Use chipped ice to make home-made ice cream.

Ice Cream

Make **ice cream** sundaes. Set up a sundae making station at one table. Place the different toppings in separate bowls. Place word labels next to each bowl. Allow the children to make their own sundaes.

Iced Tea

Let the children make **iced tea**. They can make decaffeinated sun tea. Have them use a large glass jug, fill the jug with water, place about 12 tea bags in the water and close the top. Instruct them to place the jug in a sunny window for several hours. Allow the child to discuss their observations of the tea making processes. Have a tea party! This is good time to emphasize manners.

Igloos

An **igloo** is an Eskimo house or hut that is made from blocks of snow and formed in the shape of a dome. Build **igloos** with sugar cubes and glue. Show the children a picture of an igloo in an encyclopedia or book, such as "Building An Igloo," by Ulli Steltzer, Henry Holt, 1999.

Iguana

Read a story about an **iguana**. What do they look like? What helps them blend into their surroundings?

Incense

Burn **incense** in the classroom and have the children tell about what it smells like.

Initials

Encourage each child to practice writing his/her **initials** with pencil and paper, with a stick in the sand, or with their finger in pudding or shaving cream. During attendance time, write each child's initials on the board (one at a time), ask the children to guess whose initials they are.

Insects

Learn about **insects**. All insects have three main body parts – head, chest, and abdomen. Most insects lay eggs. Their antennae are used to taste, touch, smell, and detect sound. The tiny hairs on their bodies help them to detect sound and air movement. They have an external skeleton, but no bones or skeleton. Adult insects have six legs. Most insects have wings and the ability to fly. Insects have either simple eyes or compound eyes. Insects are well adapted to the many environments in which they live. They use various methods to protect themselves. Some of these methods include blending in with their surroundings, giving off a special odor, making sounds, flashing signals, making themselves appear larger, and stingers to attack others. Some insects can be harmful to humans by spreading disease and destroying crops or buildings. Some insects are beneficial to humans by pollinating flowering plants, fruits and vegetable plants, eating harmful insects, and by providing food for other animals, including humans. Look for more interesting ideas and information in the Early Childhood Thematic Book "Bees, Bugs, and Butterflies," Teacher's Friend Publications, 2001.

Instrument

Play musical **instruments**. Make up different rhythm patterns for the children to imitate. Have a parade.

Invention

Learn about a simple **invention** (for example, the light bulb). Who made the discovery? What can people do with it? How does it help people?

Italy/Italian Bread

With a knife, spread jam on **Italian** bread and eat it. Find **Italy** on a globe. Collect menus from Italian restaurants and add them to the Dramatic Play Center. Learn about the people who live in Italy.

Other words that begin with the letter I:

These words may arise in naturally occurring conversations throughout the day/week. As you use these words, point out that they start with the letter "i" and write them on an index card to add to your word board.

icicle (outside)	**inch** (math, measurement)
identical twins (people)	**infant** (baby)
ill (sick)	**iris** (colored part of eye)
in, inside, invisible (concepts)	**ivy** (plant)

Picture Cards

ice cube

ice cream

icicle

igloo

instruments

iron

island

ivy

insects

Word Cards

iron	ice cube tray
instruments	ivy
IN sign	invitation
insects	icicle
ironing board	ice cream
igloo	island
incense	ink
initial	iguana

Trace and Write

Trace and write the letters. Color the picture.

Name

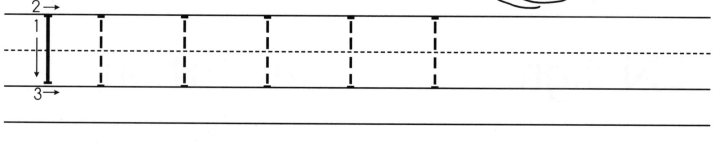

Uppercase I

2 →
1
↓
3 →

Lowercase i

1 • • • • • •
↓

Name

I am learning about the letter I i.
This is how I write it:

Here are some words that start with the letter I i:

This is my picture of an _____.

Letter J

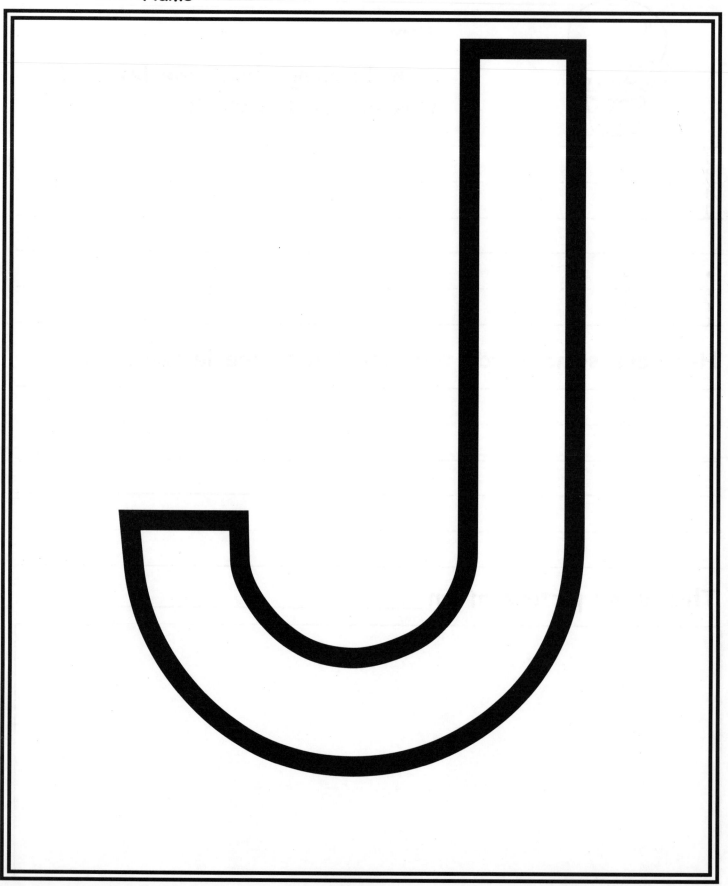

Letter j

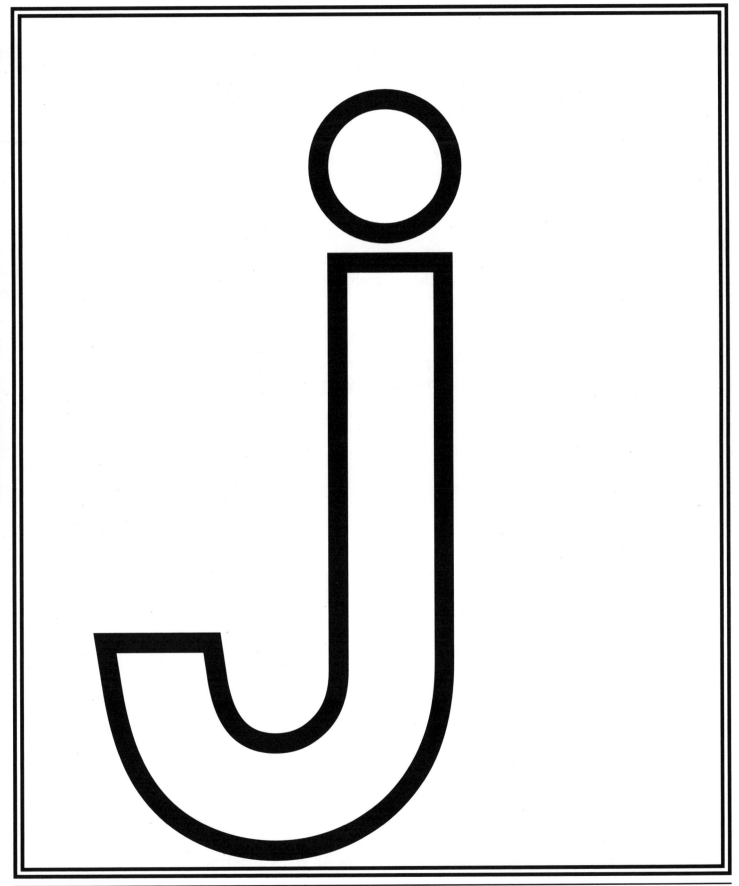

Ideas and Activities for the Letter:

Jj

Jacket
Add "J" items to the Dramatic Play Center for dress up. For example: **jackets**, **jeans**, and **jewelry**.

Jack-O-Lantern
Carve a pumpkin into a **jack-o-lantern**. Make and eat pumpkin treats (roasted pumpkin seeds, muffins, pie, cookies, etc.).

Janitor
Invite the **janitor** from your school to come into your classroom and talk about what he/she does to keep the school clean and safe. How can the children help?

Jar/Jug
Fill a **jar** or **jug** with paperclips, pennies, pom poms, buttons, marbles, or sunflower seeds.   Ask the children to guess how many items are in the jar? Count them and then identify the person who was closest.

Jeep/Jet
Play with **jeeps** and **jets** in the Building and Block Center.

Jelly/Jam
With a knife, spread **jelly** on toast for a snack.

Jiggle
Make and eat **Jello®**, Show the children how it **jiggles**.

Jigsaw Puzzle
Put together a simple **jigsaw** puzzle.

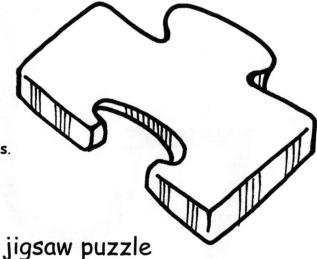

jigsaw puzzle

Job
Make a list of people's **jobs**. Start with people in the school or maybe parents' jobs. Invite parents to visit the class and discuss their jobs. Cut out pictures from magazines of people doing different jobs and display them on a board with the heading "We All Work Together."

Jockeys

Learn about **jockeys**. Jockeys are people who ride horses, usually in races. What do they do? Usually, how tall are they? Do they have to go to school to learn to be a jockey? What types of clothes do they wear and why?

Jog

Go on a short **jog** around the neighborhood, school, or park.

Journal

Ask the children to start a **journal**. At least once a week, have the children write something in their journals. They can write about something that happened to them that week, something they are thankful for, how they feel, or something that may happen to them in the future. Occasionally provide a entry starter at the top of the page such as: "I like to do many things with my family, like...."; "This is how to cook a turkey..."; "I like to _____with my best friend _____..."; My favorite thing about summer is......"; "I like to help my family by......"; "What I like best about me is.....". Make the journals very special. Have the children decorate the covers. They can draw pictures in their journals. Younger children can dictate their ideas to an older child or adult who can write them down or they can write the words themselves (inventive spelling is fine).

Juice

Make **juice** with a **juicer** or hand squeeze orange juice.

Jumping

Have the children do ten **jumping jacks** before they line up for lunch.

Other words that begin with the letter J:

These words may arise in naturally occurring conversations throughout the day/week. As you use these words, point out that they start with the letter "j" and write them on an index card to add to your word board.

January, July, June (months)
jaw (body part)
Jay (child's name or bird)
junk (trash)

Picture Cards

jacket

jack-in-the-box

jack-o-lantern

jeep

jug

jelly jar

jewelry

jigsaw puzzle

jump

Word Cards

joker	jack-in-the-box
jar	jeans
jeep	jewelry
jug	jacket
jack-o-lantern	jigsaw puzzle
juice	jacks
jet	jump rope
jelly	journal

Trace and write the letters. Color the picture.

Name

Uppercase J

J J J J J J

Lowercase j

j j j j j j

Name

I am learning about the letter J j.
This is how I write it:

Here are some words that start with the letter J j:

This is my picture of a _____.

Letter K

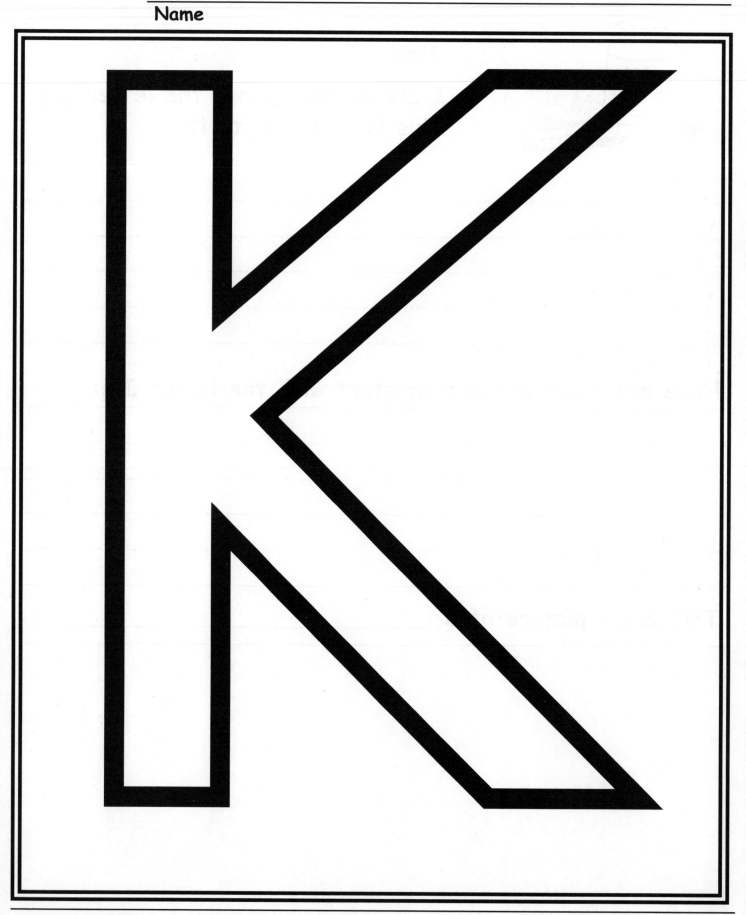

Letter K

Letter k

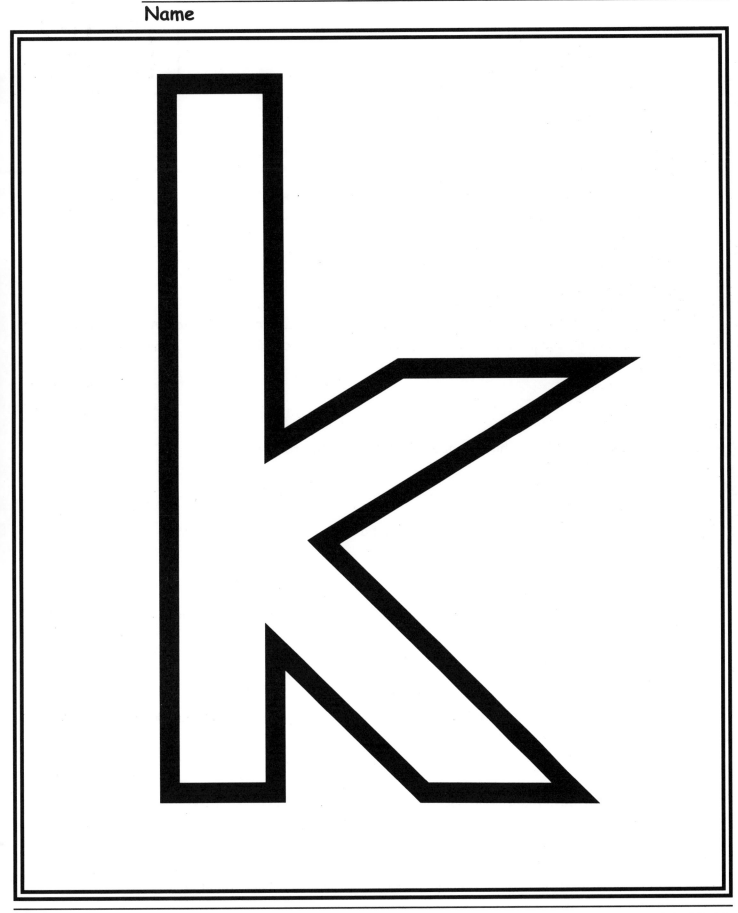

Ideas and Activities for the Letter:

Kaleidoscope
Have the children look through **kaleidoscopes**.

Kangaroo
Learn all about **kangaroos**. Kangaroos belong to the "marsupial" family. There are different types of kangaroos, such as tree kangaroos, wallabies, red, giant gray, rat, etc. They have strong back legs, huge feet, long heavy tails (to help them balance), and a pouch to carry their young. They also have excellent hearing, vision and sense of smell. Most kangaroos hop and cannot walk backwards. They eat fruit, leaves, grass and roots. Kangaroos live in Australia.

Kayak
Borrow a **kayak** from a sport center, fellow teacher or parent. Place the kayak in the Dramatic Play Center. The children can pretend they are riding in it. They can learn about some of the safety rules and equipment.

Kennel
Visit a local **kennel**. Tell the children about how to care for family pets.

Kick
Kick balls in the play yard. See who can kick the ball the farthest, highest, etc.

King/Knights
Pretend to be **kings** and **knights** in the Dramatic Play Center. Decorate the area like a castle. Make crowns in the Arts and Crafts Center.

Kitchen
Write a list of items found in a **kitchen**. List "K" food words, such as **ketchup, kiwi** fruit, **kidney** beans, etc.

Kite
Fly **kites** on a windy day. Make wind sock kites in the Arts and Crafts Center.

Kiwi Fruit
Use a **knife** to cut **kiwi** and eat it for snack. Have the children feel the peel.

Knead

Make a loaf of homemade bread. **Knead** the bread dough. Make a birdfeeder by following these steps: 1.Thaw frozen bread dough. 2. Knead the thawed dough and roll it out like a long snake. 3. Form the dough into a circle (wreath shape). 4. Bake the dough. 5. After the bread has cooled, spread peanut butter on the bread and sprinkle it with birdseed. 6. Attach a string or ribbon for hanging. 7. Hang in a tree and watch the birds eat.

Knee

Have the children create a class mural. Tape a large sheet of bulletin board paper across the lower half of a wall. Instruct the children to **kneel** on their **knees** (without sitting on their feet) and draw on the paper with colored pencils, crayons or markers. This position encourages strong back and stomach muscles as well as supports appropriate positioning of a pencil.

Knife

The children can practice using a butter **knife**. Demonstrate how to hold and use a knife with play dough. During snack time, they can use the knife to spread peanut butter, jelly, or cream cheese onto crackers, toast, or bagels.

Koala

Learn all about **koala** bears. A koala is an Australian marsupial with gray fur and hairy ears. They eat eucalyptus leaves. They are not bears.

Other words that begin with the letter K:

These words may arise in naturally occurring conversations throughout the day/week. As you use these words, point out that they start with the letter "k" and write them on an index card to add to your word board.

ketchup (food)

kids (children)

Kindergarten (class)

kitten (pet)

keys, knob, knock (on a door)

knot (practice tying shoes)

key

Picture Cards

kangaroo	kettle	keys
king	kite	kick
kitten	ketchup	kitchen

Word Cards

kaleidoscope	kettle
key	king
kite	knob
kimono	ketchup
kangaroo	kazoo
kayak	knife
keyboard	kernel
kid	kiss

Trace and Write

Trace and write the letters. Color the picture.

Name

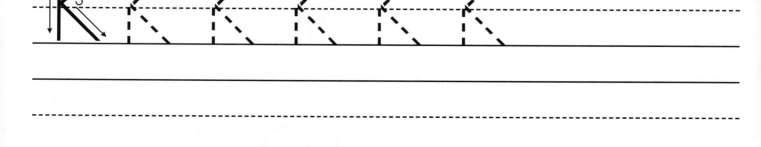

Uppercase K

Lowercase k

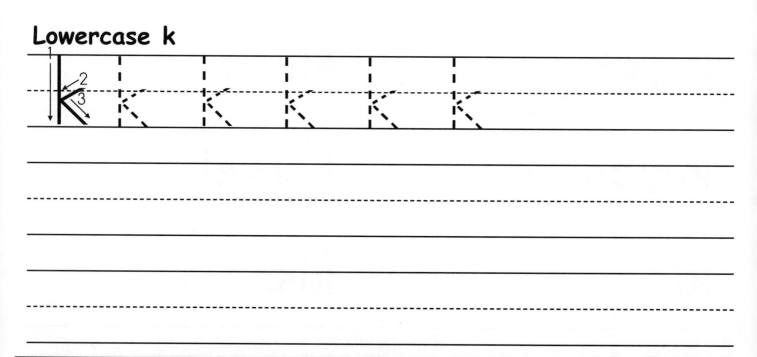

My Alphabet Book

_____

- -

_____

Name

I am learning about the letter K k. This is how I write it:

Here are some words that start with the letter K k:

This is my picture of a _____ .

Letter L

Name

Letter I

Name

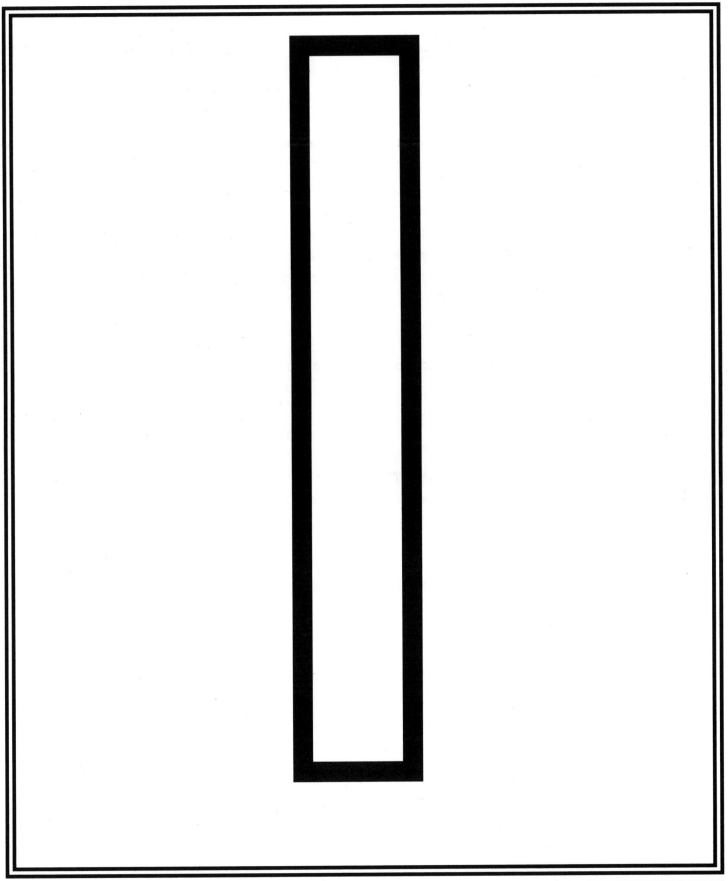

Ideas and Activities for the Letter:

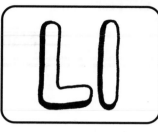

Lace
Practice **lacing** with lacing cards or shoes.

Ladle
Play a transfer game. Separate the class into two or three teams. Have the teams **line** up at the start line. Place a bucket of water and one **ladle** in front of each team. Place an empty bucket at the finish line. The first member of each team holds their ladle in their **left** hand, fills their ladle with the **liquid** and carries it to the bucket at the finish line. They pour the liquid into the buckets and race back to their teams. Then the next team members repeat the activity. The members are encouraged not to let the liquid **leak** out of the ladle. The game ends when one bucket overflows or when each member has had one turn and the team bucket with the most water wins.

Ladybug
Encourage the children to observe the **ladybugs** at the sand table. Ladybugs can be purchased at your local gardening store.

Launch
Pretend to **launch** toy rockets on the **lawn**. Many people participate in the hobby of launching small rockets. Ask one of them to your classroom to demonstrate a rocket launch.

Laundromat/laundry
Visit a local **Laundromat**. What goes on there? Who works there? What type of equipment is used?

Left
Have a **left-handed** day. Instruct the children to try to do things with their left hand. Examples of things to try: shaking hands with a friend, cutting play dough with scissors, scooping with a spoon, throwing a ball, etc.

Leg
Make a list of thing you can do with your **legs** and try them (bend, hop, jump, run, walk, wiggle, etc.).

Lemons/Limes
Add **lemons** and **limes** to water for a fresh drink. Make **lemonade**.

Length
Measure the **length** of similar items and tell which one is the **longest**. Some items you might need are: a short and **long** pencil, a short and long piece of ribbon, a short and long **line** written on a piece of paper, a short and long block, etc.

Letters
Practice writing the **letters** of the alphabet.   Provide a variety of tangible letters (magnets, foam, block, etc.) and ask the children to find the letters of their name or find all of the "L" letters. **Look** for the letter "L" in store signs, street signs and on **license** plates as you take a walk around the neighborhood.

License Plates
Have the children make **license** plate rubbings for a home activity. The children can place a piece a tracing paper over the plate and rub it with the side of a crayon. Display all of the rubbings on a board. Find similar **letters** or numbers in the plates. How many "2's" are on the plates? How many "D's" can they find?

Limbo
Do the **limbo**. Use a yardstick or broomstick. Two children hold the stick up high and the other children go underneath it with their stomachs facing upwards. After each child has had a turn, the stick is **lowered** and the activity is repeated. How **low** can they go? Play limbo music.

Lion
Learn all about **lions**. Male lions have thick shaggy manes around their heads and the females have no manes. Most male lions weigh approximately 270-500 lbs., have **long** canine teeth, and short powerful **legs** with claws. They **live** about 13 years. Lions travel in groups called "prides" which consist of 1-6 males, 4-12 females and their cubs.   Each pride has its own territory. They sleep during the day and hunt at night.

Litter
Give each child a bag and encourage them to pick up the **litter** in the play yard or at a local park. Talk to the children about the importance of keeping our neighborhoods clean and not **littering**.

Living Room

Write a **list** of items found in a **living** room.   Make sure to include such things as; **lamps, lounge chair, leather** couch, etc.

Lizard

Learn all about **lizards**.   A lizard is a four-legged scaly reptile with a **long** tail.   What do they **look like**? Where do they **live**? What do they feel like? What do they eat?

Log

Bring a **log** into your classroom. Encourage the children to explore it. How big is it? Why does it have rings and what do they mean? What does the bark feel **like**? Demonstrate how to transfer the bark's texture onto paper holding a piece of tracing paper on the bark and rubbing the side of a crayon over the paper.

Lunch

Prepare a special "L" **lunch**, serve **lasagna** and **lemonade**. Have the children help prepare the meal. Invite family members in for this special lunch.

Other words that begin with the letter L:

These words may arise in naturally occurring conversations throughout the day/week. As you use these words, point out that they start with the letter "l" and write them on an index card to add to your word board.

label (on a product or piece of clothing)

library (in classroom or school)

lift (picking up something)

light (fixture)

lips (on face)

look, listen (using eyes/ears)

loop (when tying shoes)

loud (noise)

love, lucky, laugh (related to feelings)

low, large, little, last, late (concept)

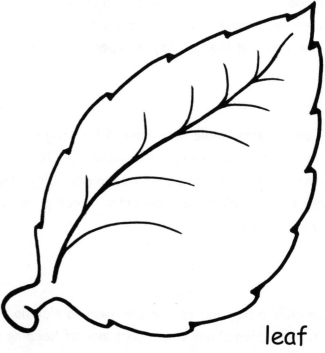

leaf

Picture Cards

log

lemon

ladder

ladybugs

lamp

lobster

lizard

letters

lion

Word Cards

lace	ladder
ladle	lantern
leash	leather
lemon	lime
lock	log
laundry basket	lobster
lamp	latch
leaf	lion

Trace and Write

Trace and write the letters. Color the picture.

Name

Uppercase L

Lowercase l

Name

I am learning about the letter L l.
This is how I write it:

Here are some words that start with the letter L l:

This is my picture of a _____.

Letter M

Name _____

Letter m

128

Ideas and Activities for the Letter:

Magnets/Magnifying Glasses
Play with **magnets** and explore using a **magnifying** glass in the Science Center.

Mail/Mailbox/Mail Carrier
Learn about the **Mail** Carrier's job. Where do they work? What type of equipment or vehicle do they use? What do they deliver?

Manners
Make a list of classroom **manners**. Discuss why we use manners. Take photographs of children using good manners. Post the list and photos on a bulletin board.   Refer to the list and pictures to remind the children to use their manners.

Map
Draw a **map** of the neighborhood around the school. Draw in important buildings and roads. Have the children help identify where their houses might be on your classroom map.

Maraca
Shake **maracas** in the **Music** and **Movement** Center. Make maracas in the Arts and Crafts Center with beans, dry noodles, or buttons inside small cups sealed with a paper cap. Tape on a tongue depressor for a handle.

March
Have the children **march** for one **minute** in place.

Material
Make a **matching** game with small swatches of **material**. Cut 2" x 4" pieces of material (two of each pattern) and glue them onto index cards. Place the cards in a box, material side facing down, and have the children take turns selecting the cards. Have the children place matching cards together.

Mayor
Invite the **Mayor** of your city or town to your classroom to talk about his/her job.

Meal

Serve an "M" **meal** during lunchtime. Some suggestions might be: **macaroni**, **milk**, **melon**, **muffin** or **melba** toast with **marmalade** and **margarine**.

Mechanic

Invite a **mechanic** into your classroom to discuss his/her job. What type of tools do they use? What type of vehicles do they fix, repair or maintain?

Melt

Fill a jug with snow or ice and watch it **melt**. How long does it take to melt (time)?

Menu

Make menus for the Dramatic Play Center. Glue **magazine** pictures of food on the inside of a file folder. Add prices. Children can decorate the covers of their menus. Add **Mexican** menus and play foods to the Dramatic Play Center.

Microphone

Invite the children to make "M" sounds into a **microphone** – cow **(moo)**, **motor** (vroom), **monkey** sounds, a **mosquito** buzzing, or a **mouse** squeaking.

Mirror

Mirrors form images by reflection. Have the children brush their teeth or hair while looking into a **mirror**. Place a large mirror or hand mirrors in the Dramatic Play Center.

Mitten

Fill a basket with **mittens** and have the children **match** them and hang them on a clothesline with clothespins.

Monkey/Moo

Have the children act like **monkeys** or cows in the **Music** and **Movement** Center.

Morning

Talk about a **morning** routine. What do you do in the morning after you get out of bed? Send home information on morning routines to families as a way to encourage a positive start to a full day of learning.

Mosaic

Help the children make **mosaics**. Give them small ceramic, plastic, felt, foam or paper tile pieces to create unique pictures or three-dimensional projects.

Moss

Look for **moss** on trees, rocks or on the ground.

Mother/Mom

Have the children write a "Thank you, **Mom**" note.

Mud

Add water to the sand table or sand section in the play yard to create **mud**. Encourage the children to **manipulate** it. Make mud pies. Observe how it drips and oozes from one's fingers.

Music

Encourage the children to **move** to **music**. Play music with different rhymes and beats. **Make** music with instruments.

Other words that begin with the letter M:

These words may arise in naturally occurring conversations throughout the day/week. As you use these words, point out that they start with the letter "m" and write them on an index card to add to your word board.

mad (feeling)

make, made, mix, mug, meat,

mayonnaise (lunch time)

many, medium, middle (concepts)

markers (art)

mat (rest or movement time)

math (subject)

May, March (months)

measure (science)

memory (game)

mess, mop (clean-up time)

Monday (day of the week)

moon, mountains (outside)

month (calendar)

muscles (body)

monkey

Picture Cards

mailbox

mask

mushroom

mittens

muffin

mouse

money

monkey

mirror

TF1432 Letter of the Week!

Word Cards

magnet	magnifying glass
maraca	mask
microscope	mitten
moss	microphone
mop	mouse
mirror	milk carton
marker	menu
metal	marble

Trace and write the letters. Color the picture.

Name _____

Uppercase M

M M M M M M M M M M

Lowercase m

m m m m m m m m m

My Alphabet Book

_____

- - - - - - - - - - - - - - -

_____

Name

I am learning about the letter M m.
This is how I write it:

M M

m m

Here are some words that start with the letter M m:

_____   _____

- - - - - - - - - - - -   - - - - - - - - - - - -

_____   _____

- - - - - - - - - - - -   - - - - - - - - - - - -

This is my picture of a _____.

Name

Letter n

Name

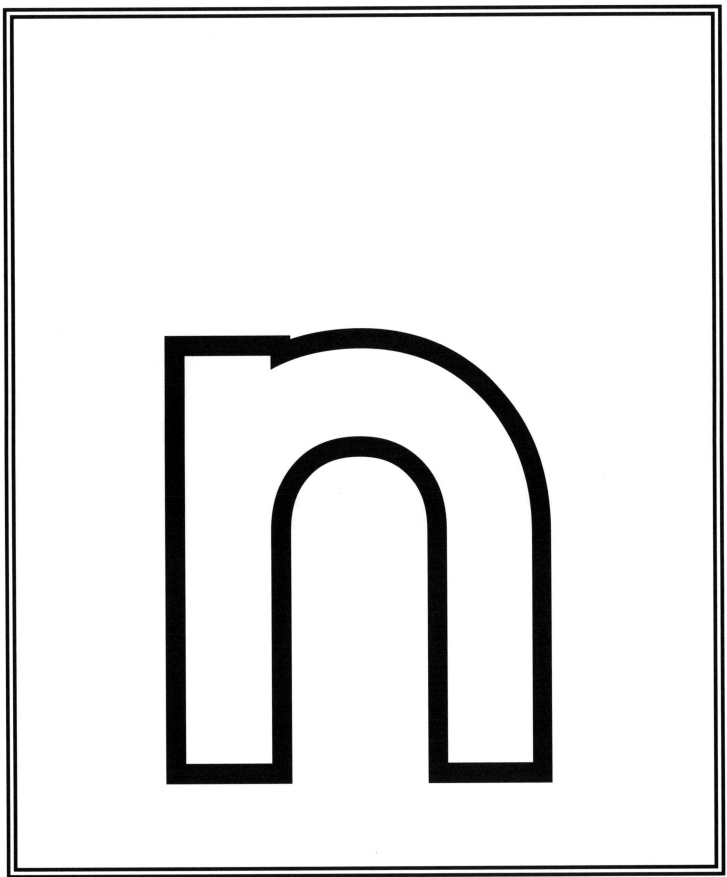

Ideas and Activities for the Letter:

Nn

Nachos
Make and eat **nachos**. Place tortilla chips or corn chips in a bowl, sprinkle with grated cheese and heat in a microwave oven.

Nails
Fill a container with **nails** and invite the children to sort them by size. Hide nails in the sand and have the children dig for them. Measure and weigh the nails.

Name
Practice writing full **names**. Make a classroom name book. Place a current picture of each child on a page with a small caption which includes the child's full name. Include a page for yourself (the teacher) as well. Arrange the pages together in a binder and place the book in the Library and Writing or Dramatic Play Center.

Napkin Rings
Make a simple set of **napkin** rings by cutting paper towel tubes into four sections and decorating them with craft materials.

Nature
Create a **nature** collage. Go on a nature walk and provide a small bag for each child. As you walk, they can collect nature items in their bags such as leaves, acorns, small stones, etc. In the Art and Crafts Center, have the children use glue, cardboard and their nature treasures to create beautiful collages.

Necklace
Make **necklaces** using string or yarn and colored beads, buttons or pasta.

Negotiate
Encourage children to **negotiate** with their peers when resolving conflicts. Start when children are young talking about **negotiating** and compromising skills.

Neighbor
Interview a known adult **neighbor**. Develop a list of three or four questions that the children can ask a neighbor. Instruct the children to go to the neighbor's home/apartment with a parent or older family member. This is a fun home activity.

Nest

Locate a real bird's **nest** and let the children examine it. Explain to them how it was made and what type of bird made it.

Net

Give the children small **nets** to play with in the play yard and watch their imagination soar. They may collect **nature** items (rocks, grass, small bugs) or they may try to pour sand through the holes, or try to catch butterflies.

New

Discriminate between **new** and old items. Fill a bag or box with the following items: a new and old sneaker, a new and old sock, a new and old toy, a new and old block, a new and old coin, a new and old book, or any other new and old objects. Invite each child to select an item and tell whether it is new or old and why. Have the children match pairs of new and old items together.

News

At the beginning of the day, offer an opportunity for the "**News** of the Day." Let the children pretend that they are **newscasters** by providing a microphone and inviting them to talk about something of their choice. You may want to prompt the children to talk about a special place they visited with their family, a restaurant they went to, the weather report for the day, an upcoming activity that they are interested in, or what they may choose to do that day during center time.

Newspaper

Create a list of different things that can be created with old **newspapers**. Have the children try some of them, such as making paper mache, rolling it into a ball, making **new** paper or cards, wrapping presents with comics, making a hat or airplane, etc.

Nickel

Count **nickels** (by 5's) to equal one dollar.

Nickname

Talk about **nicknames**. Discuss how some nicknames are acceptable while others are hurtful. Talk about where nicknames come from, such as a shortened version of a first or last name (John or Johnny), initials (JP), or related to something that describes the person or his/her activities (Big Joe). Have the children come up with nicknames that they might like to be called.

Nighttime

Talk about a **nighttime** routine. What do you do in the nighttime before you go to bed? Send home information on nighttime routines to families as a way to encourage a positive end to a full day of learning.

Nine

Count **nine** "N" items: **nails, nuts, necklaces, neckties, napkins, nickels.**

Noisemakers

Have the children blow, shake, or spin **noisemakers.**

Nose

Make a list of all the things that you can smell with your **nose.**

Numbers

Play games with **numbers** (bingo, memory, crazy eights, etc.) Use number magnets and blocks in the Math and Manipulatives Center.

Nurse

Invite a **nurse** to visit the classroom and talk about his/her job. Where do they work? How do they dress? What equipment do they use?

Nuts

Sort and count **nuts.** Press nuts into clay or play dough. Weigh nuts on a scale.

Other words that begin with the letter N:

These words may arise in naturally occurring conversations throughout the day/week. As you use these words, point out that they start with the letter "n" and write them on an index card to add to your word board.

nap (rest time)

nervous, nice (related to feelings)

next, not, now, narrow, never, no, none, neither (concepts)

November (month)

Picture Cards

nest

net

necklace

nickel

newspaper

nail

nuts

needle

nine

Word Cards

nail	napkin ring
napkin	necklace
nest	net
nylon	nuts
nickel	nozzle
noisemaker	newspaper
noodles	numbers
nurse	necktie

Trace and Write

Trace and write the
letters. Color the
picture.

Name _____

Uppercase N

N N N N N N

Lowercase n

n n n n n n

My Alphabet Book

Name CA

I am learning about the letter N n.
This is how I write it:

Here are some words that start with the letter N n:

This is my picture of a _____ .

Letter O

Name

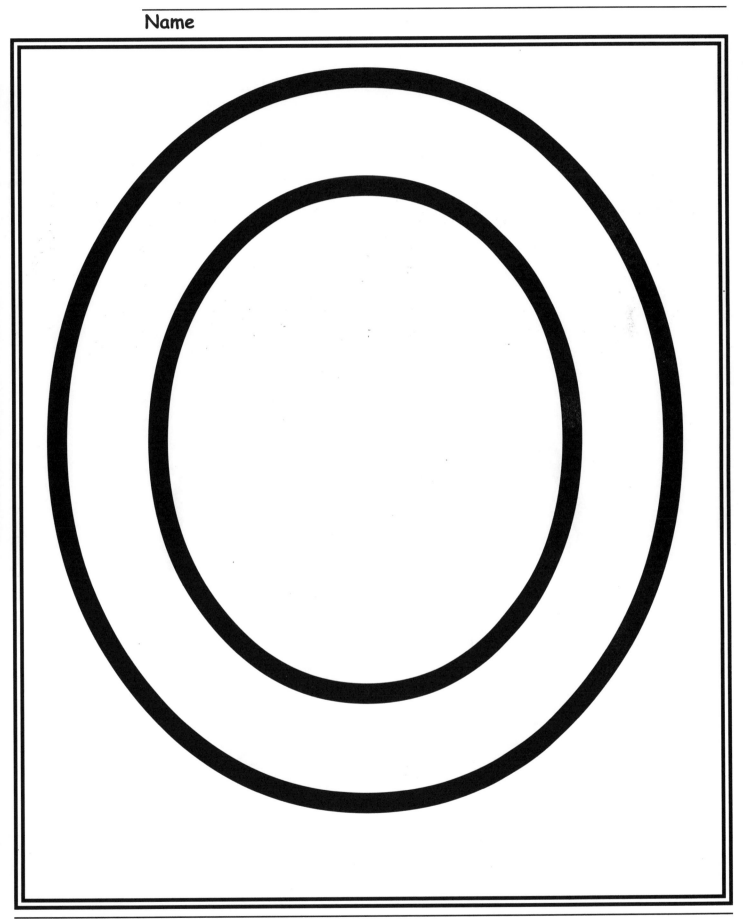

Letter o

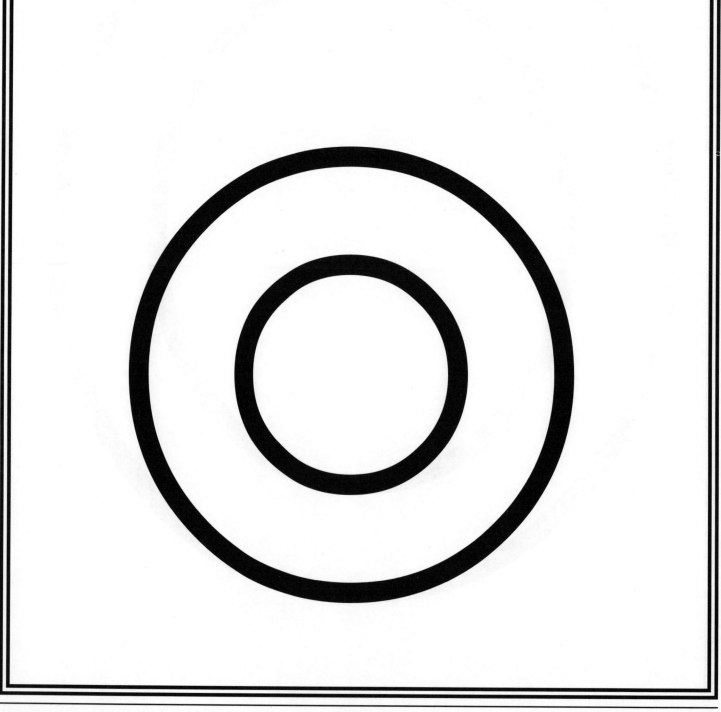

 TF1432 Letter of the Week!

Ideas and Activities for the Letter: Oo

Oatmeal
Serve **oatmeal** for breakfast or a snack. Add jam, honey, cinnamon or raisins.

Obstacle Course
Navigate an **obstacle** course. Build an obstacle course in your large motor area or **outside**. Include obstacles that require the children to go **on, over**, under, and through. You will need items such as hoola hoops, tires, mats, low balance beams, tunnels, low trampoline, cones, etc).

Octagon/Oval
Copy an **octagon or oval onto** construction paper and demonstrate how to cut it **out**. Have the children count the number of sides in the octagons.

Octopus
Learn all about the **octopus**. This soft-bodied sea creature has eight large tentacles with suckers. They use the suckers to stick to rocks, catch food, and move along the ocean floor. Make a craft octopus using a small paper lunch bag stuffed with tissue paper and eight paper streamers to represent its tentacles.

Odor
Bring in different things that smell (soap, candles, spices, coffee grounds, etc.). Tell the children that the way something smells is its **odor**. Have the children smell the items and talk about the odors that they smell.

Old
Fill a large garbage bag with **old** items such as an old sneaker, an old toy, an old banana, an old pencil, an old newspaper, an old book, and an old pair of pants. As each one is removed from the bag, identify it as being "old." Talk about: Why the item is old? What makes it look old?

Omelets
Serve **olive** and **onion omelets** for a special snack/breakfast.

One

Find the number **"one"** in things around the classroom. Hint: on the clock, in toys or games, on product boxes in the Dramatic Play Center, in books, on the computer, on the calendar, etc.

Orange

Peel an **orange** and eat it. Cut a circle from orange paper and make an orange collage with orange items, such as paper, yarn, ribbon, crepe paper, pom poms, etc.

Orchestra

Listen to **orchestra** music. Learn about the different instruments that are played in an orchestra.

Ornament

Make an **orange ornament**.   Ask students to decorate an orange with whole cloves by poking the cloves into the flesh of the orange. Attach a hanging ribbon to the top of the orange with a couple of toothpicks. Hang the aromatic orange in the classroom. Encourage the children to describe the smell (odor).

Outdoors/Outside

Make list of fun things to do **outside** or **outdoors**. Send the list home to families. Encourage them to spend time outside every day.

Other words that begin with the letter O:

These words may arise in naturally occurring conversations throughout the day/week. As you use these words, point out that they start with the letter "o" and write them on an index card to add to your word board.

October (month)

over, on, out (concepts)

octopus

Picture Cards

octopus	oar	ostrich
owl	oil can	orange juice
ornament	onion	oatmeal

Word Cards

oatmeal	oar
octopus	orange
onion	ornament
oven	outlet
open sign	owl
oval	orchid
oak leaf	overalls
orange juice	

Trace and Write

Trace and write the letters. Color the picture.

Name _____

Uppercase O

Lowercase o

My Alphabet Book

Name

I am learning about the letter O o.
This is how I write it:

Here are some words that start with the letter O o:

This is my picture of an _____ .

Letter P

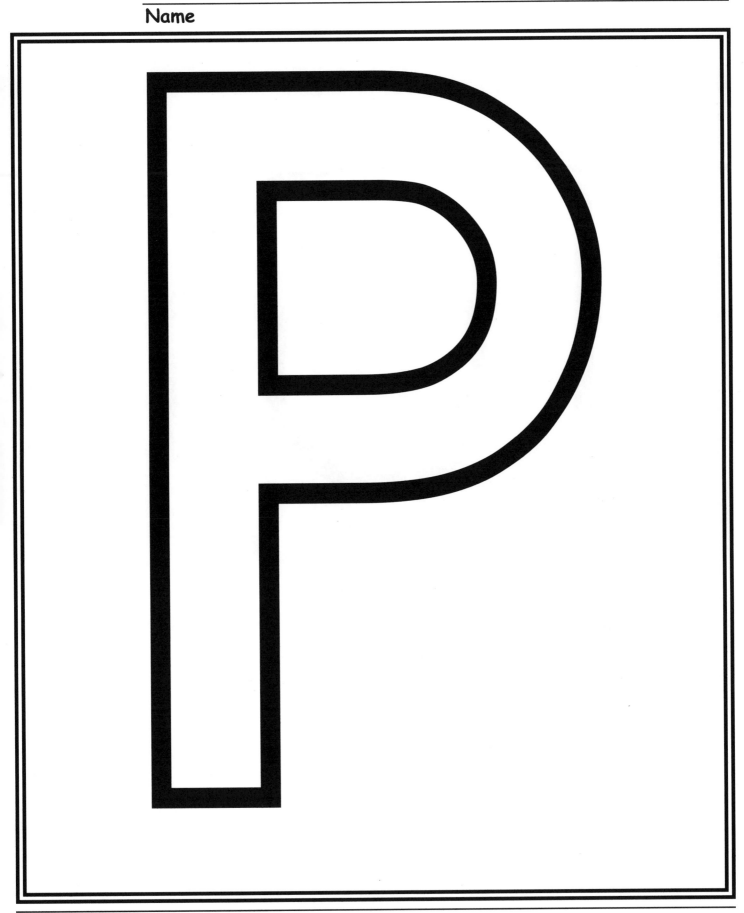

Letter p

Name

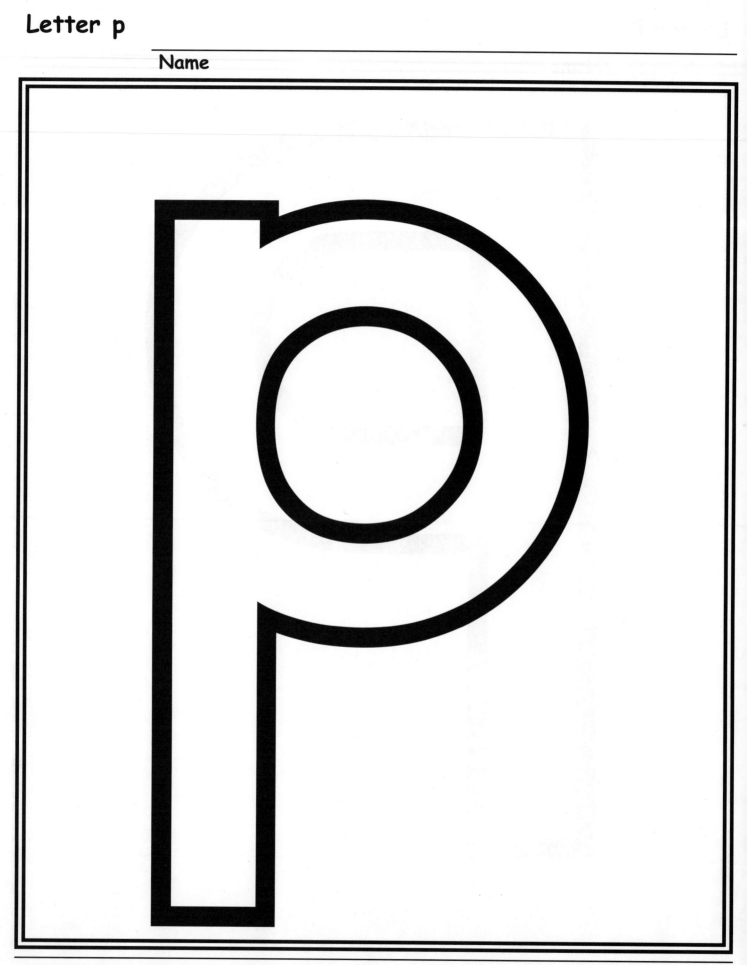

154

Ideas and Activities for the Letter: **Pp**

Pack
Make a list of things you might **pack** for a **picnic**. Bring in a picnic basket with all the items. The children can pretend to go on a picnic in the Dramatic Play Center or you can take the class on a real picnic.

Package
Make a "care" **package** for children in a hospital or elderly patients in a retirement home. Arrange to have the children deliver them, if possible.

Painter/Paintbrushes/Pail
Provide **painter** hats, large **paintbrushes,** and **pails** full of water. Instruct the children to pretend to be painters by **painting** (with water) the brick or concrete walls or fences on the outside of the school.

Pairs
Make a list of things that come in **pairs**, such as sandals, boots, sneakers, shoes, mittens, gloves, hands, feet, eyes, ears, arms, legs, socks, thumbs, earrings, twins, pants, etc.).

Pancakes
Make and eat **pancakes**. Read the story "Pancakes, Pancakes" by Eric Carle.

Paper
Name all the things that you can do or make with or to **paper**. Then try some of them, such as: make an airplane or hat, draw a picture, write a letter or note, cut, color, paint, or fold it.

Paperclip
How many words can you make from the letters in **"paperclip"**? Show the children that the words paper, clip, lip, pear, real, cap, cape, lap, a, I, ripe, pal, are, rap, etc. can all be made from the word paperclip. You may also want the children to link paperclips together to make a chain.

Parachute
Play games with a colorful **parachute**. Many commercially sold parachutes have great ideas in their **packages**.

Partridge

Learn about birds that begin with the letter "P." Examples: **partridge, parrot, peacock, pelican, penguin, pheasant, pigeon,** and **puffin.** Look for more interesting ideas and information in the Early Childhood Thematic Book "Feathered Friends," Teacher's Friend Publications, 2001.

Pea Pods

Remove **peas** out of **pods.** (This is a good fine motor task.) Enjoy the peas for snack.

Pegboards

Manipulate **pegs** on a **pegboard.** Make different **patterns.** Have the children create their own patterns and then replicate them.

Penny

Have each child place several **pennies** in the **palm** of his/her hand. Ask the children to count the pennies by transferring the pennies from one palm to the other.

People

Learn about **people** from a different state, country, or culture.

Pepper

Bring in variety of "P" things that smell – **pepper** mill (grind pepper), **peppermint** candy, **petunia, perfume, potpourri, powder,** and **pine** tree branches. Encourage the children to use their sense of smell to explore the items.

Periscope

Play with **periscopes.** Have students **pretend** to be on a submarine in the Dramatic Play Center.

Pet

Make a **pet** chart. Ask the children to each tell about their family pets. Record the type and number on the class board. Add the number of cats, dogs, hamsters, and other pets once the chart is complete.

Petal

Place a variety of flowers or **petals** from flowers in your empty water table. Encourage the children to explore the petals. Ask about the many different sizes, colors, and shapes of the petals. Keep a written list of their discoveries. **Press** the petals between wax **paper** or contact paper to make beautiful bookmarks or **placemats**.

Piano

During quiet/rest time, listen to **piano** music.

Pig

Pigs are long round-bodied farm animals. They have short legs, short bristles, **poor** eyesight, a sharp sense of smell, and a snout. They are raised on farms for meat, leather, glue, soap, fertilizer, and medicine. Pigs like to lie in the mud to cool off. They live in **pens** called sties. Make pig **paper** bag **puppets**.

Pizza Party

Serve **pizza** from a **platter** on **purple** or **pink plastic** or **paper plates**. Serve with **popcorn**, **pretzels**, **pistachio pudding**, and a **pitcher** of **pink** or **purple punch**.

Please

Count the number of times **people** say **please** in one day.

Pledge of Allegiance

Encourage your children to recite the **Pledge of** Allegiance. "I pledge allegiance to the flag of the United States of America, and to the Republic for which it stands, one nation under God, indivisible, with liberty and justice for all."

Police Officer

Invite a **Police** Officer into your classroom to discuss his or her job. What do they do? Where do they work? How do they help us stay safe? What can we do to help the police officer do his or her job?

Polka Dots/Pleats/Pockets/Plaid

Add **polka** dotted, **pleated**, **pocketed**, or **plaid pants**, hats, socks, shirts, skirts, scarves, and other dress-up items to the Dramatic **Play** Center.

Postcards

Collect **postcards** and **place** them in the Library and Writing Center. Have the children create their own postcards and mail them at the **Post** Office.

Pound

What weighs one **pound**? Use a scale and teach the children how to read the large numbers. Weigh and count "P" items (**pennies, pencils, paperclips, pegs, paper**). Families can weigh vegetables and fruits on the grocery store scale in the **produce** section.

Present

During attendance, count how many **pupils** are **present** or absent for each day. Are there more children present or absent?

Principal

Invite your school **principal** into your classroom to talk about his/her job.

Prism

Explore **prisms**. Light is refracted as it **passes** through the prism. Can the children see the rainbow?

Prize

Play a game and give "P" **prizes**. Wrap them like **presents**. Here are some ideas: **puzzle, purse, puppet, powder, pencil**, and **pad** of **paper**. Many of these items can be **purchased** at a local variety or dollar store.

Produce Party

Have a **produce tasting party**. What types of foods are found in the produce section of the grocery store? Make a list. How many start with the letter "P"? Sample a few of them, such as **peppers, pickles, pineapple, pea pods, pumpkins, potatoes, plums, prunes, peaches**, and **pears**.

Purple

Emphasize the color **purple** in the following ways: Squirt a few tablespoons of red **paint** and a few tablespoon of blue paint into a **plastic** zip type bag. Close the bag tight. Encourage the children to manipulate the bag and discover what happens when they mix the two colors together. Dance with purple scarves. Cut out shapes from purple construction paper.

Pussy Willows
Bring in **pussy willows** for the children to explore.

Puzzle
Separate the classroom into **partners** (teams of two). **Provide** a floor **puzzle** for each team and instruct them to work with their partner to complete the puzzle.

Pyramids
Display **pictures** of **pyramids** in the Blocks and Building Center. Encourage the children to use different types of blocks to build pyramids. Take picture of them with their creations and display them in the same area.

Other words that begin with the letter P:
These words may arise in naturally occurring conversations throughout the day/week. As you use these words, point out that they start with the letter "p" and write them on an index card to add to your word board.

pastels (Arts and Crafts Center)
pen, pencil (Library/Writing Center)
push, pull, put (concepts)

pig

Picture Cards

pail	pancakes	parrot
penguin	pie	pineapple
pig	pumpkin	pyramid

TF1432 Letter of the Week!

Word Cards

paddle	pail
pan	pillow
pocketbook	postcard
price tag	prism
powder	pumpkin
pussy willow	puzzle
puppet	potato
plunger	platter

Trace and Write

Trace and write the letters. Color the picture.

Name

Uppercase P

P P P P P P

Lowercase p

p p p p p p

My Alphabet Book

Name

I am learning about the letter P p.
This is how I write it:

P P

P P

Here are some words that start with the letter P p:

This is my picture of a _____ .

Letter Q

Name

Ideas and Activities for the Letter:

Quack
Have the children **quack** like ducks as a transition activity.

Quart
Add **quart** containers and plastic bottles to the water or sand table to fill and pour.

Quarter
Have the children do **quarter** rubbings. Tape quarters onto a piece of cardboard. Cover the quarters with tracing paper. Demonstrate how to rub the side of a crayon over the paper to expose the quarters. Quarters can also be pressed into play dough to make impressions. Sort the new state quarter coins and discuss the pictures on the quarters.

Queen
Add "**queen**" type clothes and costumes to the Dramatic Play Center (crowns, scarves, frilly dresses, high heeled shoes, etc.).

Queen Anne's Lace
Add the wild flower **Queen Anne's Lace** to the Art and Crafts Center. Use the flowers to make several art projects.

Quiche
Help the children made and eat a simple **quiche**. You will need: one refrigerated pie dough circle, 6 to 8 eggs, diced up ham or vegetables, grated cheese, salt, pepper, and milk. Place the pie dough circle (crust) into a pie pan. Beat the eggs and combine all ingredients before pouring the mixture into the crust. Bake the quiche at 400 degrees until the mixture is firm.

Quiet
Talk about **quiet** time. What should everyone be doing during quiet time? (Resting/napping, looking at a book, whispering, listening to soft music) Why do we need a quiet time each day? (To rest, for good health) What types of things help us relax and enjoy quiet time? (Soft music, a blanket or stuffed animal, a mat or soft place to lie down)

Quilt

Make a classroom **quilt**. Show the children a real quilt and point out the pieces and shapes used to put together the pattern of the quilt. Give each child a 6 inch square of construction paper. Provide a variety of shaped pieces of construction paper, markers, and glue. Ask each child to make a "quilt" square to add to the classroom quilt. Have each child write his or her name on the front of their square. Arrange the quilt squares into a pattern and display it on a bulletin board.

Other words that begin with the letter Q:

These words may arise in naturally occurring conversations throughout the day/week. As you use these words, point out that they start with the letter "q" and write them on an index card to add to your word board.

quarrel, quiver, quit (related to emotions),

quick (concept)

quiet

Picture Cards

| question mark | quilt | quarter |
| queen | quart | quacking |

Word Cards

| quilt | quarter | Queen Anne's Lace |
| quart | queen | question mark |

Trace and Write

Trace and write the letters. Color the picture.

Name _____

Uppercase Q

Lowercase q

My Alphabet Book

Name

I am learning about the letter Q q.
This is how I write it:

Here are some words that start with the letter Q q:

This is my picture of a _____.

Letter R

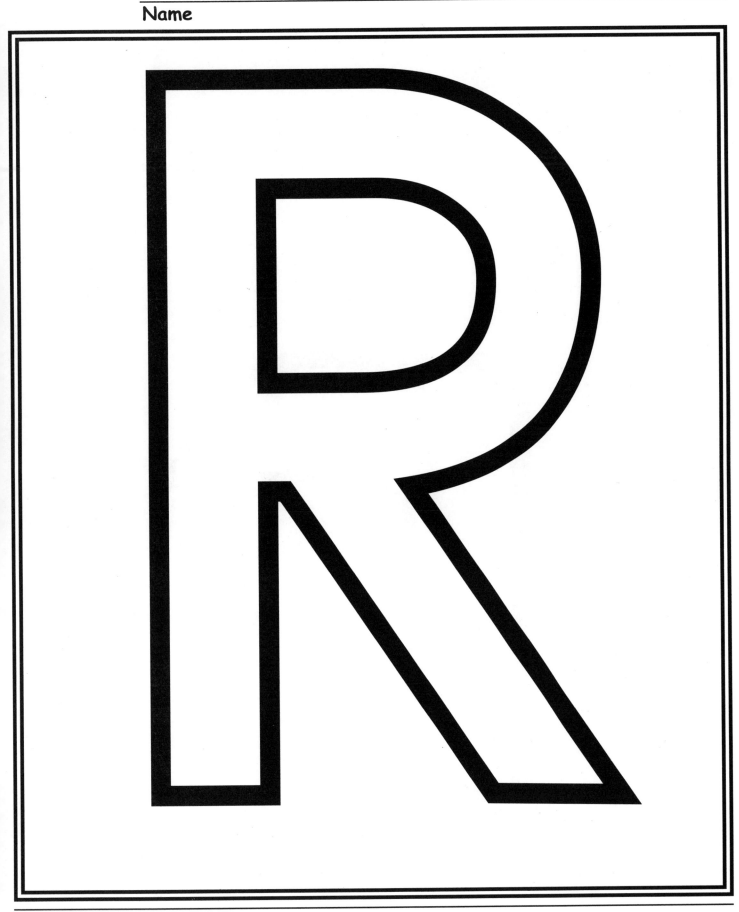

Letter r

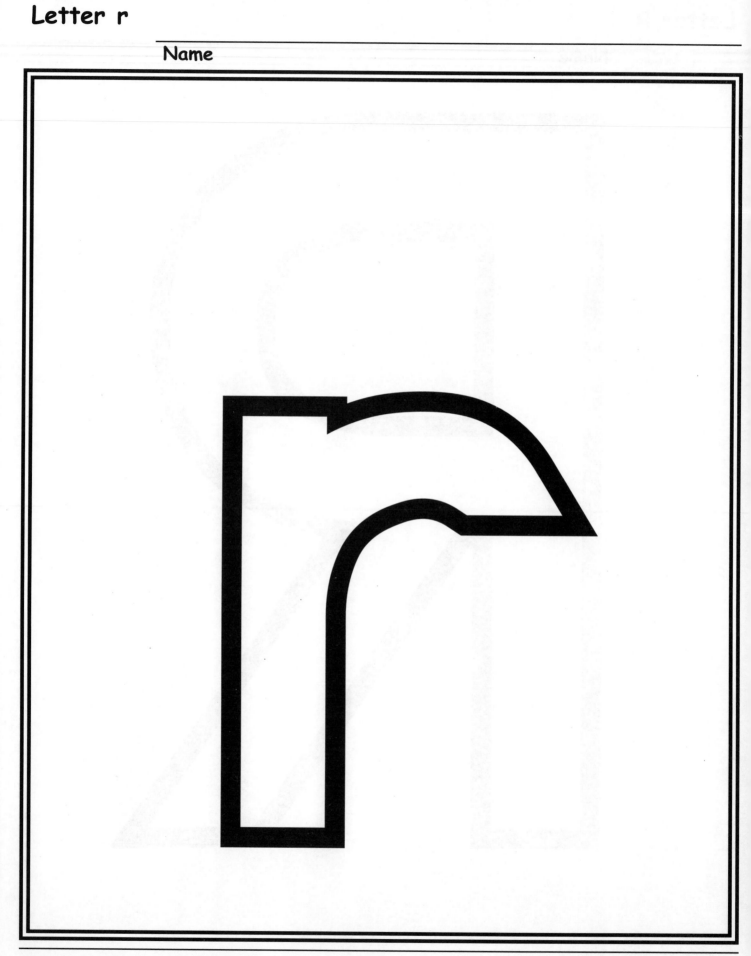

172

Ideas and Activities for the Letter:

Raisins

Make **raisins** by placing **red** grapes in a food dehydrator. Open the dehydrator periodically so that the children can observe the process. Let the children eat the raisins during snack time.

Rearrange

Rearrange the **room** before the children arrive. During morning circle, ask the children to look around the room and describe the things in the room that have been rearranged.

Recipe Cards

Send blank **recipe** cards home and ask families to submit their child's favorite recipe. Compile all of the recipes and make a book to share with the families. Keep a few copies of the book or the recipe cards in the Dramatic Play Center.

Record

Record the children **reciting** their favorite song into a tape **recorder**. Play the tape back and ask the children to guess who is singing.

Red

Look around the classroom. How many things can you find that are **red**? Place several red items in the explore tub. Make a red collage with red scraps of material, crepe paper, tissue paper, **ribbon**, pipe cleaners, pom poms, etc. Add red food coloring to milk to make a red drink. Eat red foods for snack (strawberries, apples, cherries, **raspberries**, dried cranberries, red Jello®). Paint with red finger paint.

Reflection

Pass a mirror to each child. Ask each one to look at their **reflection**. What do they see in the mirror? Children may name face parts or may discuss what type of friend or person they are.

Refrigerator

List things found in a **refrigerator**. Ask the children to name "**R**" types of foods, such as **relish**, **raspberry** jam, **root** beer, **radishes**, etc.

Relax

Talk to the children about how they may feel when they are upset or tired. Ask how their body might feel (wiggly, tense) and what they might be doing (whining, crying, stamping their feet, yelling). Talk about different ways to **relax** when you are upset, tired or excited.

Repair Shop

Set up a **Repair** Shop in the Dramatic Play Center. Include tools, clipboards, old small appliances with cords **removed**, and tool belts.

Restaurant

Collect menus from different **restaurants** and add them to the Dramatic Play Center. Have the children play the **roles** of people in a restaurant (waiter, chef, customer, etc.). Include some of the following items: tablecloths, aprons, chef hats, menus, placemats, silverware, plates, cash **register**, order pad, pencils, and food trays.

Ribbon/Rubber Bands/Rubber Stamps

Add different types and colors of **ribbons, rubber** bands, and **rubber** stamps to the Arts and Crafts Center and discover all of the creative things that the children can make with them.

Rice

Fill a bucket or an empty water table with dry **rice**. Add scoops, ladles, spoons, measuring cups and containers and watch the children pour, measure, and compare.

Ride

Have the children **ride** tricycles, bikes, and other outside **riding** equipment. Create a simple course with cones and count the number of times that each child rides around the course.

River/Road

Collect a variety of small vehicles that can either go in a **river** or on a **road**. Place them in the Blocks and Building Center. Encourage the children to sort them by where they are **ridden**.

Roar

Have the children **roar** like lions.

Rocks

Collect a variety of **rocks** (**round**, glittering, **rough**, smooth, different colors) to add to the Manipulatives Center.   **Record** the words that the children use to describe the rocks on a piece of paper and post it near the center.

Rolling pin

Use **rolling** pins with play dough. Small wooden dowels can be purchased at a local hardware store and cut into rolling pin size.

Roots

Place a variety of **roots** (carrots, **radishes**, beets, plant roots, a large tree root) in the Science Center for exploration.

Rough

Collect a variety of **rough** and smooth items. Place the items in a bag. Invite each child to **remove** an item and describe it as either "rough" or "smooth." Sort the items into rough and smooth piles.

Round

Read to the class the book "What is **Round**," by Rebecca Kai Dotlich, Scholastic Inc., 1999. Find or name things that are round. Place the round items in the explore tub.

Routine

Take pictures of the children throughout the day. Display the pictures in sequence depicting the **routine** of day.

Other words that begin with the letter R:

These words may arise in naturally occurring conversations throughout the day/week. As you use these words, point out that they start with the letter "r" and write them on an index card to add to your word board.

relative (family)
rest, **reward** (related to feelings/emotions)
right, **rectangle**, **remove**, **repeat** (concepts)
rinse, **ripe** (cooking)
roll, **run**, **race** (music and movement time)
ruler (art or math)

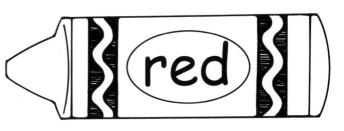

Picture Cards

radio

rainbow

rabbit

rock

rocking horse

roller skate

rooster

rolling pin

refrigerator

Word Cards

racquet	radio
raft	rattle
register	recipe cards
ribbon	robe
rolling pin	rose
rubber band	rubber stamp
ruler	rope
rake	rabbit

Trace and write the letters. Color the picture.

Name

Uppercase R

R R R R R R

Lowercase r

r r r r r r

Name

I am learning about the letter R r.
This is how I write it:

R R

r r

Here are some words that start with the letter R r:

This is my picture of a _____ **.**

Letter S

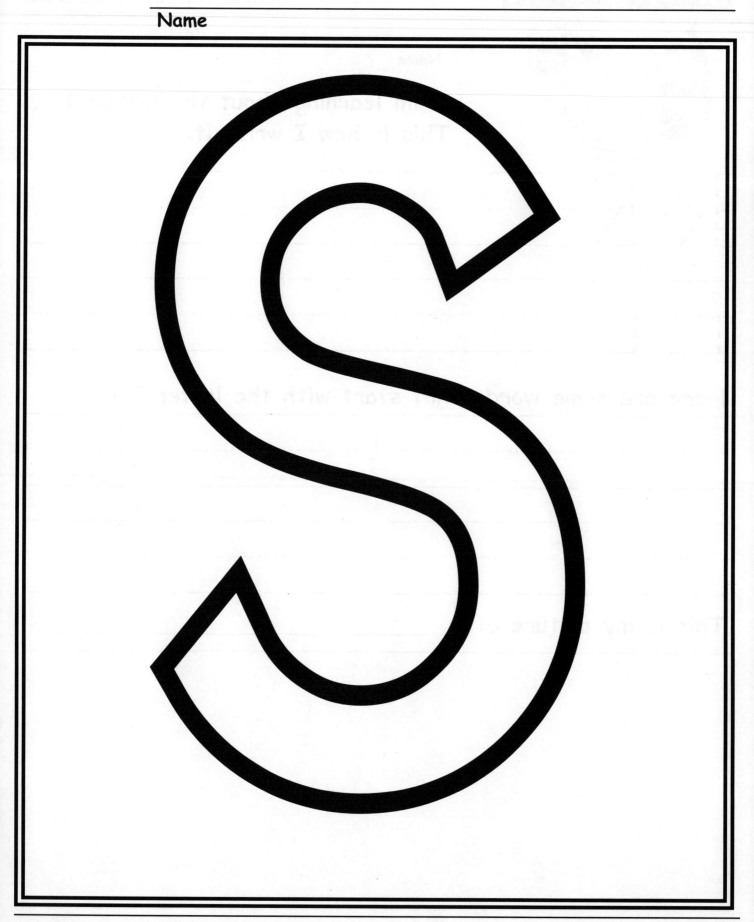

Letter s

Name

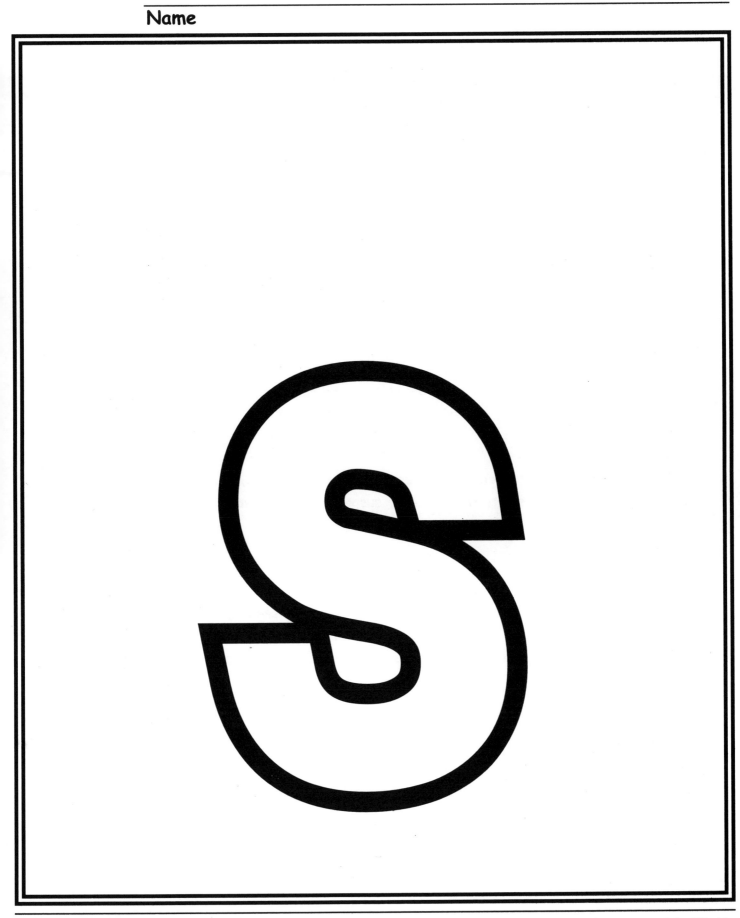

Ideas and Activities for the Letter:

Salad

Help the children create a classroom **salad**. Ask each family to send in one item to add to the salad. Let the children tear the lettuce, cut tomatoes and cucumbers (using a plastic knife), mix the dressing, etc. Count the number of each ingredient. Weigh the ingredients on a **scale**. Eat the salad during lunch or **snack** time.

Scale

Find things that weigh **six** or **seven** pounds. How many blocks (or rocks or **shoes**) does it take to weigh 6 or 7 pounds? Use a digital **scale** and fill a paper bag with the items that you are weighing. Children can make predictions, then conduct the activity, and discover the answer. Help the children identify the numbers on the scale. Find other things in the room to weigh on the scale.

Scarecrow

Help the children build a **scarecrow** using old clothes and rumpled newspaper.

Scarf

List "S" things that we wear: **sneakers, shoes, sandals, sunglasses, socks, shawl, slippers, smock, skates, sombrero, shirt, skirt, scarf, suspenders.**   Add **some** of these things to the Dramatic Play Center.

Scavenger Hunt

Conduct an "**S**" **Scavenger** Hunt. Make this a home activity by **sending** the list home and having the child and parent initial next to the items that they find. Ideas for the list might be: **sachet,** toy **sailboat,** ice cream **scoop, scarf, sandal, scissors, seven** cents, **stapler, sneaker, sock, shampoo, soap, soup.**

Scents

Provide a variety of things that **smell**. Make **small sniff sacks** using **squares** of cheesecloth and tying them with **string**.   Include things such as a **sachet** (potpourri), **scented soaps, and spices.**

Schedule

Talk about the **schedule** for the day. What comes first, in the middle, and at the end of the day. Take photographs of the children throughout the day. Ask the children to **sequence** the pictures to depict the schedule for the **school** day.

Scratch

Give the children **scratch** and **sniff smell stickers** for rewards.

Sea

Learn about all of the things related to the **sea** that **start** with the letter "S": **squid**, **shrimp**, **shells**, **sand**, **scallop**, **snail**, **starfish**, **ships**, **seashore**, **shark**, **seal**, **submarine**, **surf**, **snorkel** and/or **scuba** diver, and **swimming**. Look for more interesting ideas and information in the Early Childhood Thematic Book "Ocean Adventures," Teacher's Friend Publications, 2001.

Seeds

Help the children plant flower or vegetable **seeds**. You may want to collect a variety of empty **seed** packets and **sort** them by type of plant or vegetable.

Shadow

On a **sunny** day, take the children outside onto a **sidewalk** or paved **surface**. Instruct the children to trace each other's **shadows** with sidewalk chalk.

Shake

Demonstrate how to make a **strawberry shake**. Place two or three **scoops** of vanilla or strawberry ice cream into a blender. Add a few strawberries and a little milk before blending. Help the children pour the shake into paper cups. Let them enjoy drinking the shakes with a **straw**.

Shapes/Square

Find, name, and explore different **shaped** objects that **start** with the letter "S": square: **sandwich** cut into **squares**, **square stencil**; circle: **slice** of **salami**, **soccer** ball, **soup** bowl; triangle: **sailboat's sail**, **sandwich** cut into triangles. Read the book "What is Square?" by Rebecca Kai Dotlich, **Scholastic** Inc., 1999

Shepherd

Learn about **shepherds** and what they do (tend and raise **sheep**). How do they **shear** their sheep? What do they do with the wool?

Signs

Display pictures of different types of **signs** (traffic or road signs, restaurant signs, exit/entrance signs, **store** signs, etc.) in the Blocks and Building Center. Talk about the signs. Where do the children **see** these signs? What do they mean?

Sky

Learn about all of the things related to the **sky** that start with the letter "S": **sun, stars, snow storm, streak** of lightning, **smog,** etc.

Slippers

Play the Great **Slipper** Race. Fill a basket with slippers. **Separate** the class into two teams. Have the children remove their **shoes.** Mark the **start** line with masking tape and place the basket of slippers across the room from the start line. The first member of each team **skips** to the basket and finds a matching pair of slippers. The child puts on the slippers and then returns back to his/her team. The next team member then goes to the basket to find a matching pair of slippers and repeats the procedure until all members of one team have slippers on and are back at the start line.

Snacks

Each day **serve** an "S" snack: **Swiss** cheese on crackers, **strawberry** jelly **spread** on toast or bagels, **strawberry sherbet, salad,** and **spaghetti.**

Snakes

Learn all about **snakes.** They are reptiles without a shell. They have long bodies, no legs, and move by **slithering** on their bellies. They have no eyelids (eyes are covered with clear **scales**) and no ear **slits** (they "hear" **sound** by feeling the movement of the air), and long forked tongues which help them **smell.** They eat only a few times a year and eat their prey whole. **Some** snakes are harmless (garter snakes) and some snakes are poisonous (rattlesnakes). Some snakes lay eggs and some give birth to their young live. Rattlesnakes have venom. When they attack, the venom is released through their fangs. Rattlesnakes have a section on the tip of their tails that makes a rattle or buzzing sound. As snakes grow, they **shed** their **skin**. Visit a pet **store** and let the children experience real snakes.

Snapping

Encourage the children to try **snapping** their fingers. Use this activity as you transition to **sit** down during circle time or when lining up to go outside.

Snip
Have the children **snip** paper with **scissors**.

Snow
Make a list of things to do in or with **snow** and then do some of them (**sleigh** or **sled** ride, **ski**, roll snow into **snowballs**, make a **snowman**, watch snow melt, walk through deep snow, dig with **shovels** in the snow, fill buckets with snow, etc.).

Soccer Balls
Let the children kick **soccer** balls. Who can kick the ball the farthest or highest?

Sole
Make **shoe sole** rubbings. Ask the children to remove their **shoes/sneakers**. Hold a piece of thin paper over the sole of the shoe and rub the **side** of a crayon across the paper to reveal the design of the sole. Display the rubbings on the class board.

Sounds
Make different **sounds**: **snort, snore, splash, squeak, sneeze**. Using a partition or box, conceal **several** items (aluminum foil, paper lunch bag, bell, plastic wrap, instruments, etc.). One at a time, take each item and produce a sound. Ask the children to guess what item is making the sound?

Sparrow/Stork/Swallow/Swan
Learn about birds that start with the letter "S": **sparrow, stork, swallow, swan**.

Spiders
Learn about **spiders**. Spiders are **small**, eight-legged animals that **spin** webs. They use their webs to catch insects for food. **Some** spiders are poisonous, but most are not. They are helpful because they eat harmful insects.

Sponges
Encourage the children to play with **sponges** at the water table or in a tub of water. Provide containers to **squeeze** the water into.

Sports

Name as many different **sports** as you can. After the list is complete, draw a circle around the sports that begin with the letter "**S**": **soccer, swimming, skateboarding, skiing, sledding.**

Stair/Steps

Count the number of **stairs** or **steps** as you walk up or down them.

Stars

Have the children cut **star shapes** from yellow construction paper. Let the children write their names on the stars and add **silver** or gold glitter.   Display the stars on the class board under the title "Our Little Stars!"

Stencil

Use **stencils** with colored pencils in the Arts and Crafts Center. Other "**S**" items to add to this area are: **sandpaper, scissors, sequins, string, sponges, streamers, sticks, stapler** and **staples, stamps,** and **scrolls** of paper. Encourage the children to create unique **sculptures** with tubes and cardboard or clay.

Stomp

Instruct the children to **stomp** their feet as they transition to the next activity.

String

Have the children **string** beads or buttons onto **shoelaces**.

Swing/Slide/Seesaw

Have the children play on the **swings, slide** and **seesaw** on the playground.

Other words that begin with the letter S:

These words may arise in naturally occurring conversations throughout the day/week. As you use these words, point out that they start with the letter "s" and write them on an index card to add to your word board.

Saturday, Sunday (days of the week)

September (month)

seven, seventeen, six, sixteen (numbers)

sing, songs (music)

soft, smooth, small (concepts)

spring, summer (seasons)

stomach, spine, shoulder (body parts)

Picture Cards

sailboat

sandwich

sink

snowflake

seal

soap

seven

socks

six

Word Cards

sachet	saddle
sandpaper	scissors
sequins	seeds
shells	screwdriver
shoelaces	shovel
silk	soccer ball
stethoscope	stones
straw	stapler

Trace and Write

Trace and write the letters. Color the picture.

Name _____

Uppercase S

S S S S S S

Lowercase s

s s s s s s

My Alphabet Book

Name

Name

I am learning about the letter S s.
This is how I write it:

S S

s s

Here are some words that start with the letter S s:

This is my picture of a _____ .

Letter T

Name

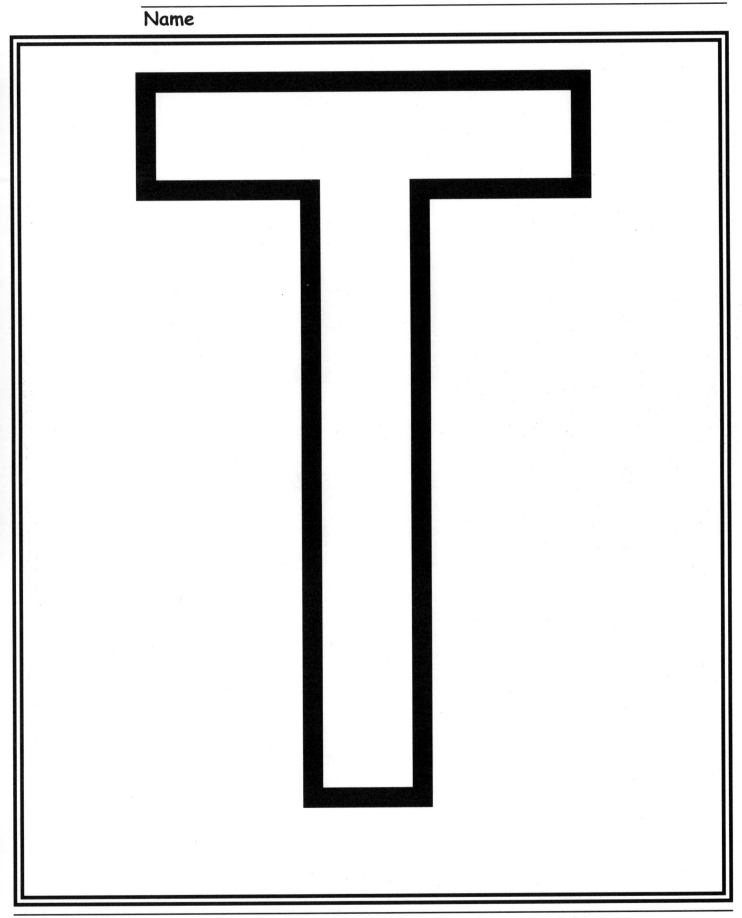

Letter t

Name

Ideas and Activities for the Letter:

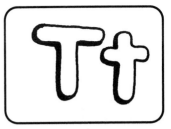

Table
Have the children set the **table** for a meal. Show them how to properly do it.

Tacos
Make and eat **tacos** family-style. Provide a taco shell for each child. Separate the ingredients (meat, cheese, lettuce, **tomatoes**) into separate bowls and allow the children to make **their** own tacos.

Tadpole
Collect or purchase **tadpoles** and keep them in a **tank** in the Science Center for observation.

Tails
Look **through** books with pictures of animals with different **types** of **tails**. What do animals use **their** tails for? (**to** swim, for balance, to swat insects, to hold **things**, to hang from **trees**) Why are **they** shaped the way they are? Do all tails feel the same? Sort the pictures by tail type (smooth, spiky, long, short, fat, **thin.**)

Tambourine/Trumpet/Trombone/Triangle
Bring in real instruments for the children to play (**tambourine, trumpet, trombone, triangle**). Children may like to make their own tambourines from paper plates stapled **together** with dried beans inside. Invite an older student who plays a trumpet or trombone to visit the classroom and demonstrate how to play the instrument.

Tape/Tear
Add "T" items to the Arts and Crafts Center: **tape, tinsel, thread, tissue** paper, and **twine**. **Tear** construction paper or tissue paper into small pieces and make a collage.

Telephone
Place an old **telephone** in the Dramatic Play Center along with a couple of telephone books. Encourage the children to pretend to **talk** to each other on the telephone. Have the children practice dialing their own telephone number. **Teach** each child how to answer the phone and respond to a phone call.

Television

Challenge yourself and your families to not watch **television** for a night or weekend. Make a written list of all the things the families did instead of watching television.

Tent/Teepee

Set up a **tent** or **teepee** outside or in the Dramatic Play Center. Let the children pretend to have a camp out.

Textures

Collect a variety of items with different **textures**. Place the items into a bag or box. Ask the children to **take turns** reaching in the bag for an object. Ask the children to describe the items they feel. Record the adjectives on a large sheet of paper with the heading "textures."

Thank You

Have the children make **Thank You** notes or cards in the Library/Writing Center.

Throw/Toss

Throw beanbags or **tennis** balls into a laundry basket. Separate the group into pairs and have them **toss** a beanbag back and forth without dropping it. Which **team** can toss the beanbag the most **times** or for the longest time?

Tic Tac Toe

Teach the children to play **Tic Tac Toe**.

Tiger

Learn all about **tigers**. Tigers have orange and black stripes making a unique pattern just like a human fingerprint. **Their** stripes make them hard to see in grasslands and jungles. **They** have long canine **teeth**, sharp claws **that** retract when not attacking prey, and excellent vision and hearing. They weigh between 350 and 600 lbs. They live about 20 years and are found only in Asia. **There** were once eight subspecies of tigers, but only five remain: Bengal, Siberian, Sumatran, Indochinese, and South China.

Tiles

Have the children make a picture or **trivet** with small ceramic **tiles**.

Time
Ask the children to measure the **time** it takes to brush their **teeth**, go to art class, get ready to go home, or any number of **things** that happens **throughout** the day.

Tiptoe
Have the children **tiptoe** around the classroom between **transition** activities.

Tomorrow
Make a list of **things that** the children **think** they might do **tomorrow**.

Tools
Read the book, "Tools" by Susan Canizares, Scholastic, Inc. 1999. Bring in the real **tools** described in the book: pliers, **tape** measure, hammer, screwdriver, ruler, wrench, drill, saw, and scissors.

Toothbrush/Teeth
Provide a **toothbrush** for each child and show them how to brush their **teeth** properly. Old toothbrushes can be used to paint with in the Arts and Crafts Center.

Tortoise
Read a version of the classic story "The **Tortoise** and the Hare."

Towers
Display pictures of **towers** in the Blocks and Building Center. Invite the children to create their own towers. Take photographs of their towers and display them alongside the other pictures.

Trace
Make individual name cards for each child in your class and place them in the Library/Writing Center. (Laminate them for durability.) Have the children **trace** the letters in their name.

Traffic Safety Rules
Instruct the children about **Traffic** Safety Rules. Look at the following websites for interesting information on this topic:

www.pbs.org   www.safekids.org

www.roadsafety.net/EDUCATIONRESOURCES/educresource.html

Transportation

Make a list of different forms of **transportation**. When the list is complete, circle the vehicles that start with the letter "T": **train, tow truck, tricycle, truck, tractor, trailer, trolley, taxi.**

Treasure Trunk

Fill a **treasure trunk** (foot locker) with "T" **treasures**, such as **tools, towel, tongs, tweezers, tennis** balls, **tray,** etc. Add other objects that do not begin with the letter "T" and ask the children to sort the objects by beginning sound ("T" and the "other letter").

Tubes

Collect a variety of **tubes** (**toilet** paper, paper **towel**, wrapping paper, etc.) and place them in the Blocks and Building Center with small cars and balls. Watch all the fun!!

Typewriter

Place an old **typewriter** in the Library/Writing Center. Encourage the children to try to spell their names with it.

Other words that begin with the letter T:

These words may arise in naturally occurring conversations throughout the day/week. As you use these words, point out that they start with the letter "t" and write them on an index card to add to your word board.

thin, thick, tough, top (concepts)

thumb, throat, toe, tongue (body parts)

today, tomorrow, Tuesday, Thursday (calendar)

tomato, tapioca pudding, turnip, toast, tuna, tortilla (foods)

trains, trucks (Blocks and Building Center)

trunk (i.e., elephant, tree, car)

twirl, twist, turn (music)

twister, tornado, tropic, thunder (weather)

Picture Cards

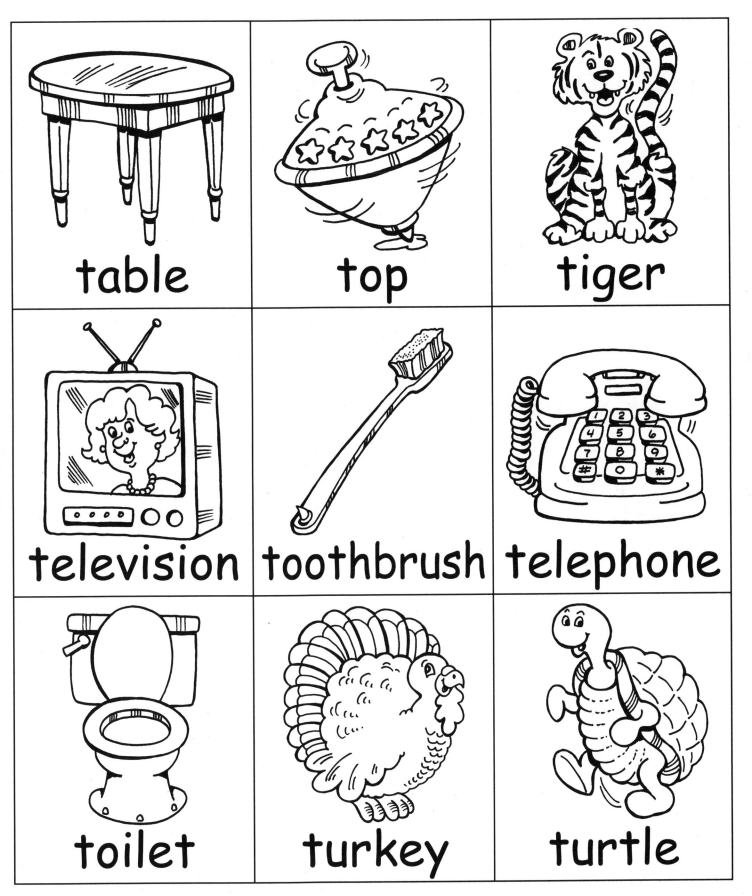

table	top	tiger
television	toothbrush	telephone
toilet	turkey	turtle

Word Cards

tadpole	tank
tambourine	tape
tennis ball	tent
television	tongs
train	twig
typewriter	tweezers
truck	twine
table	trumpet

Trace and Write

Trace and write the letters. Color the picture.

Name

Uppercase T

Lowercase t

My Alphabet Book

Name

I am learning about the letter T t. This is how I write it:

Here are some words that start with the letter T t:

This is my picture of a _____ .

Letter U

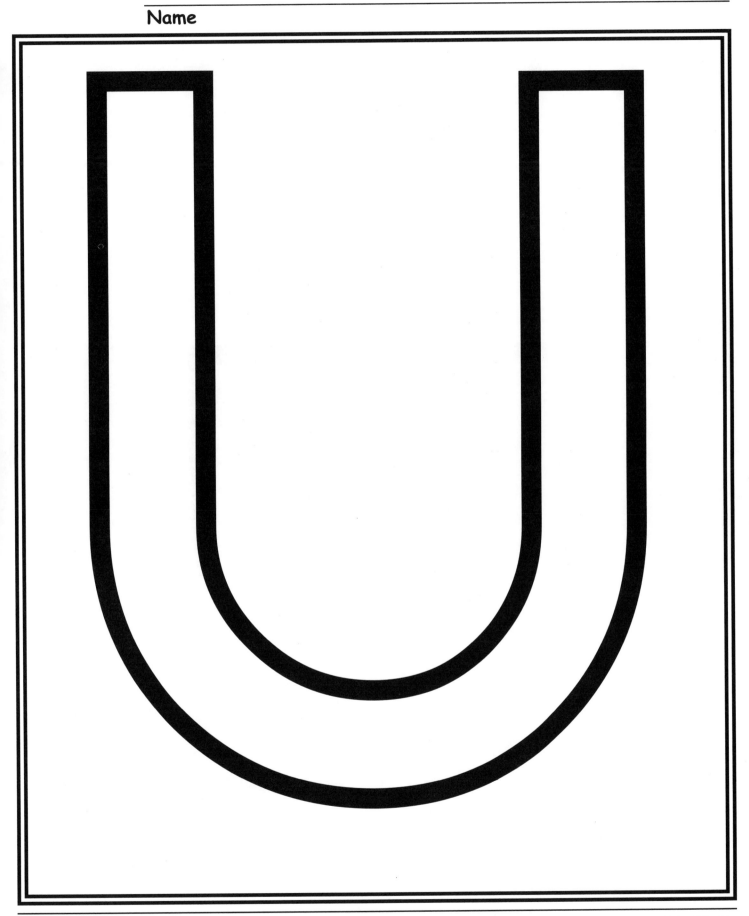

Name

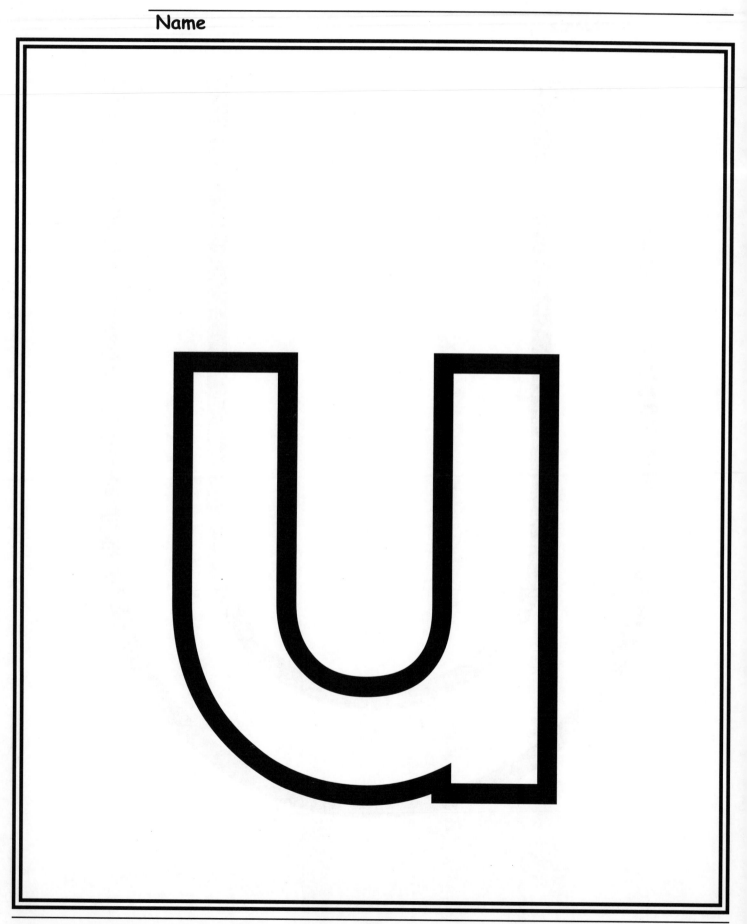

Ideas and Activities for the Letter:

Uu

Ukulele
Bring a **ukulele** to class and let the children play it.

Umbrella
Take an **umbrella** to school on a rainy day and have the children dance in the rain.
Serve the children a fruity drink and put a cocktail **umbrella** in it for decoration.

Uncle
Have the children write a special note to an **uncle**.

Under/Underneath
Let the children discover what playground equipment they can crawl **under**. Create an obstacle course in which the children must crawl **underneath** several items.

Undress/Untie
Have the children practice their dressing and **undressing** skills during arrival time, departure time, and in the Dramatic Play Center with dress-up clothes. Teach them to tie and **untie** their shoes.

Unicycle
Invite someone with a **unicycle** to come to your class and demonstrate their talent.

Uniforms
Various jobs or occupations require people to wear **uniforms**. Make a list of different occupations that require uniforms (mechanics, nurses, doctors, police officers, fire fighters, garbage collectors, chefs, football players, baseball players, etc.).

Upset
Encourage the children to talk about things that **upset** them. How does it feel to be upset? What can you do to feel better?

Utensil
Provide a variety of different **utensils**. Invite the children to sort the utensils by type. Set the table with the utensils placed correctly.

Other words that begin with the letter U:
These words may arise in naturally occurring conversations throughout the day/week. As you use these words, point out that they start with the letter "u" and write them on an index card to add to your word board.

uncover, unload (removing something)

underarm (body part)

up, upside down, upstairs (concepts)

umbrella

Picture Cards

ukulele

umbrella

umpire

unicorn

utensils

up

Word Cards

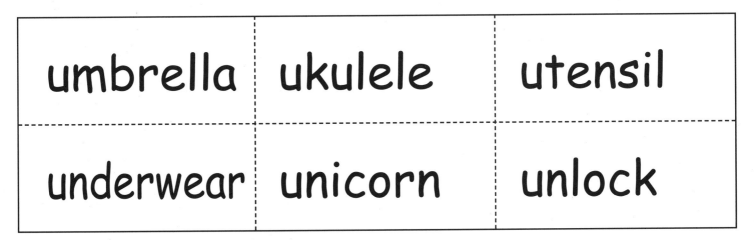

umbrella	ukulele	utensil
underwear	unicorn	unlock

TF1432 Letter of the Week!

Trace and write the letters. Color the picture.

Name _____

Uppercase U

U U U U U U

Lowercase u

u u u u u u

My Alphabet Book

Name

I am learning about the letter U u.
This is how I write it:

Here are some words that start with the letter U u:

This is my picture of an _____ .

Letter V

Name

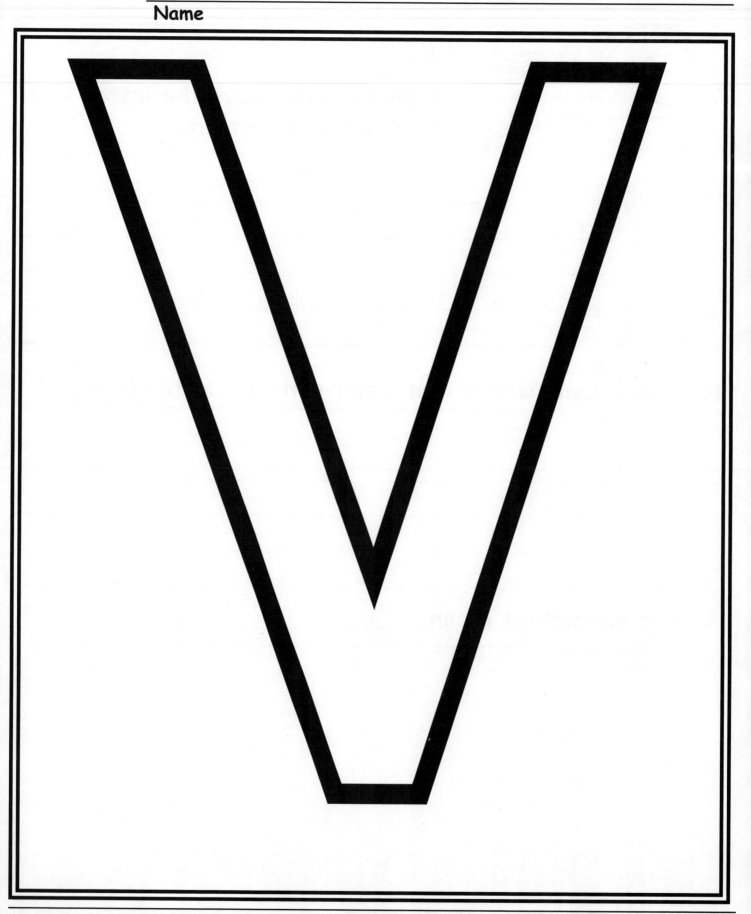

Letter v

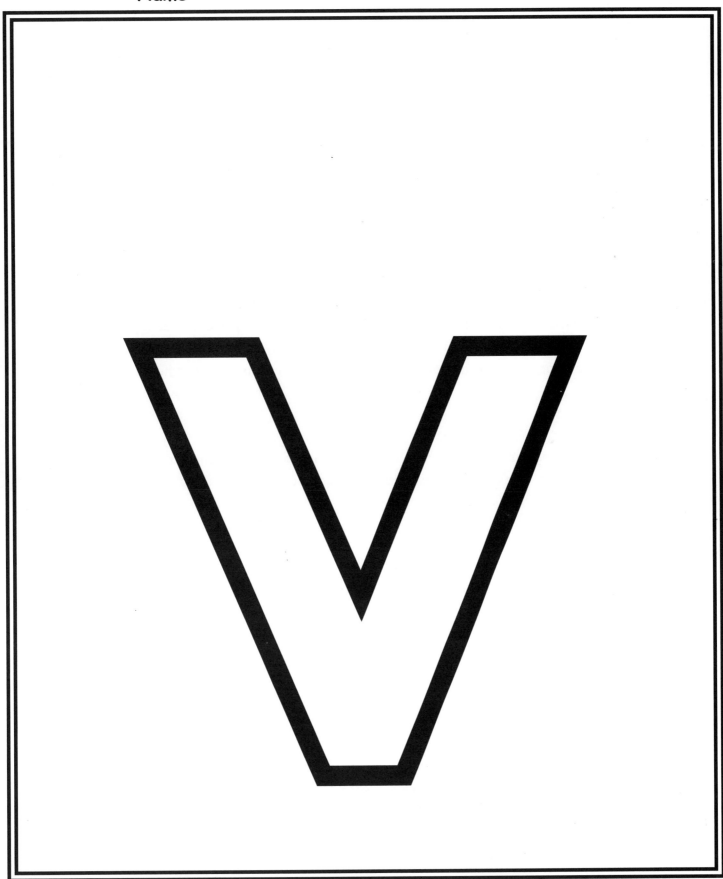

Ideas and Activities for the Letter:

Vacation
Ask the children to tell about a favorite or recent **vacation**. They may wish to bring items to school from their vacation to show to the group.

Velour/Velvet/Vinyl
Cut swatches of **velour**, **velvet**, and **vinyl** and add them to the Arts and Crafts Center. The materials can be explored, as well as used for craft projects.

Vase
Help the children make **vases** using canning jars. Mix a small amount of water with glue. Cut different colored tissue paper into small squares. Demonstrate how to dip a brush into the watery glue and paint it on the outside of the jar. Place the tissue paper squares randomly onto the jar and then paint the jar with more watery glue. Continue until the entire jar is covered. Let the jar dry thoroughly. Add plastic, silk or real flowers and display by a window or send home as a special gift.

Vegetable
Purchase a variety of **vegetables**. Ask the children to wash and sort them. Talk about the different sizes, shapes, and colors. Weigh the vegetables on a food scale. Peel and eat the vegetables for a snack.

Vehicle/Vessels
Play with **vehicles** and **vessels** in the water table or in the Blocks and Building Center.

Ventriloquist
Check you local telephone book for a **ventriloquist**. Invite him/her to perform for the class.

Veterinary
Take your children for a **visit** at a **veterinary** clinic. Learn about the many ways they help pets and what kinds of pets they help. Let the children pretend to be **vets** in the Dramatic Play Center. Include these items: vet medical kits, old white men's dress shirts or smocks, stuffed animals (dogs, cats, birds, etc.), pet food containers/boxes, collars, leashes, pet toys.

Violets

Show the children how to press **violets** between the pages of a heavy book. (Use white tissue paper to protect the pages from staining.) Place several heavy books on top and wait about two weeks. Remove the petals from the book and use them in an art project.

Voice

Demonstrate the different ways one can use his or her **voice**. Also, explain the types of places or situations in which one should change his or her voice (whisper at a library or movie, shout or yell at a sports game, inside voice while playing in the classroom).

Volcano

Learn about **volcanoes**. Show the children pictures of active volcanoes.

Volunteer

Invite parents or family members to be classroom **volunteers**. Invite them to share a hobby or their jobs, read a story, prepare a special snack, or assist on a field trip. Thank the volunteers for their time with a brief note from the children.

Vote

Invite the class to **vote** on issues that can have multiple choices (name of a class pet, which book to read first, which song to sing first, what to eat for a snack).

Other words that begin with the letter V:

These words may arise in naturally occurring conversations throughout the day/week. As you use these words, point out that they start with the letter "v" and write them on an index card to add to your word board.

Valentine's Day (holiday)

van (vehicle)

video (television)

violin (music)

vocabulary (words)

volleyball (movement)

Picture Cards

vacuum	van	vase
vegetables	vest	violin
volcano	valentine	video cassette

TF1432 *Letter of the Week!*

Word Cards

vanilla bean	vanilla extract
valentine	veil
vest	violin
vinyl	velvet
visor	volleyball
vacuum	vegetables
vinegar	vine
vase	violet

Trace and Write

Trace and write the letters. Color the picture.

Name _____

Be Mine!

Uppercase V

V V V V V V V

Lowercase v

v v v v v v

Name

I am learning about the letter V v. This is how I write it:

Here are some words that start with the letter V v:

This is my picture of a _____.

Letter W

Name

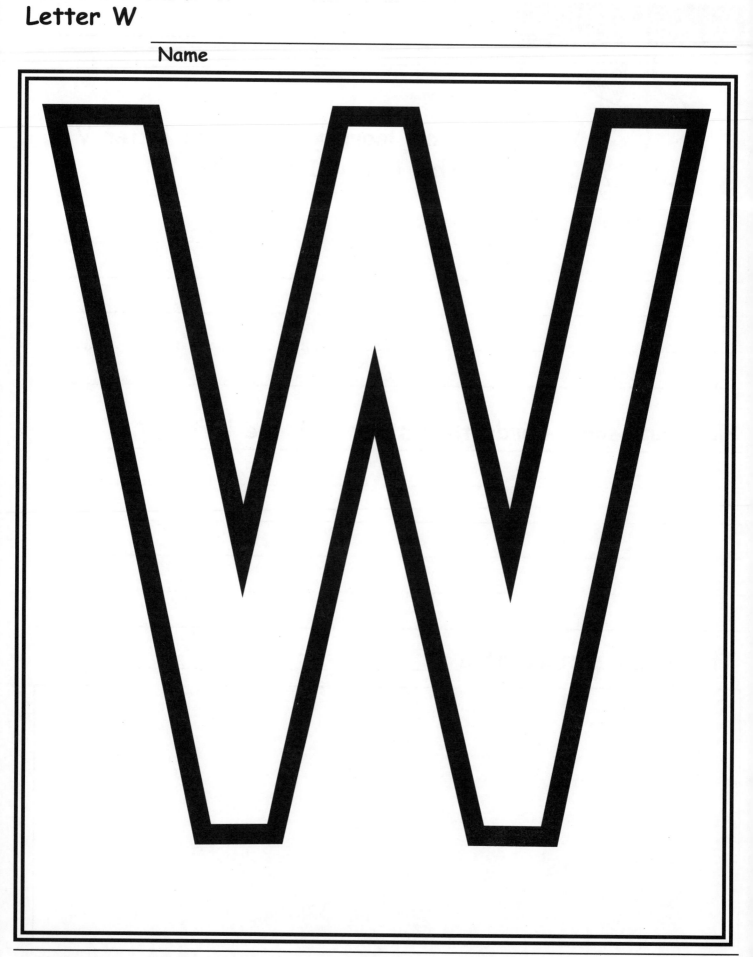

Letter w

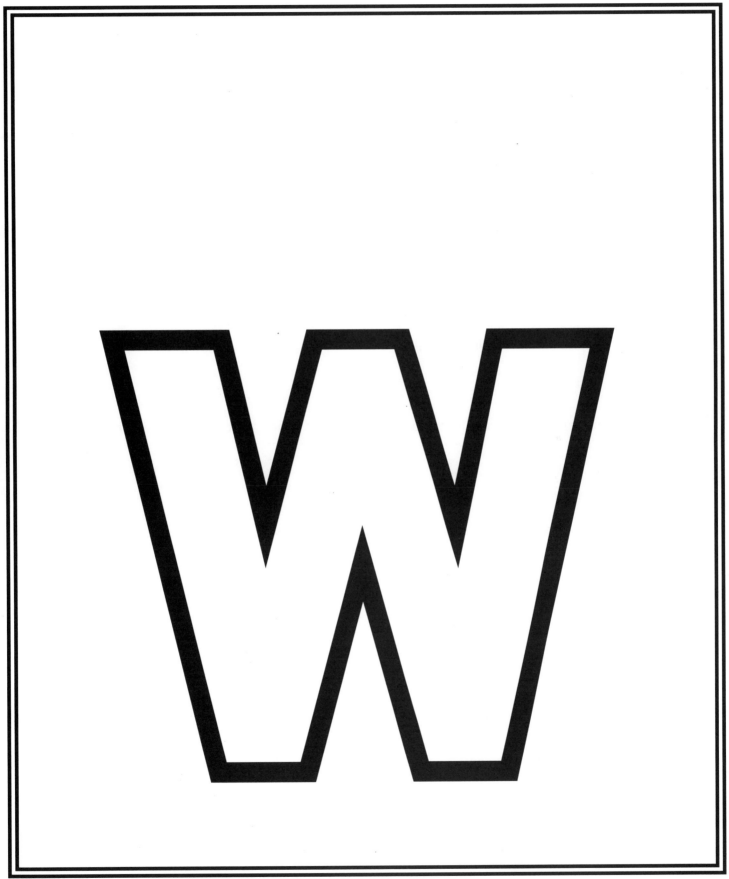

Ideas and Activities for the Letter:

Ww

Walk
Talk a **walk** with the children and look for the letter "W" in store signs, street signs, on mailboxes, in license plates, etc.

Wallet/Watch/Wedding Dress/Wig/White Wool Sweater
Add **wallets**, **watches**, a **wedding dress**, **wigs** and **white wool** sweaters to the Dramatic Play Center for dress-up.

Walnut
Have the children press **walnut** shells into clay or play dough.

Walrus
Have the children make **walrus** paper bag puppets.

Waltz
During quiet time, let the children listen to **waltz** music or dance to it at the Music and Movement Center.

Wand
Use a "magic" **wand** to transition the children from one activity to another. You can purchase a wand at a costume shop or make one by adding colorful streamers to a paper towel tube that has been covered with colorful contact paper.

Want/Wish
Make a list of things children **want** or **wish** they had.

Water
Have the children make a list of things that people can do with **water** (**wash** hands, brush teeth, wash clothes, water plants, get energy for electricity, float in a boat, wash dishes, clean food, drink it, etc.).

Watering Can
Have the children use a **watering** can to **water** plants or just to play with outside.

Watermelon

Cut **watermelon** into **wedges** and give them to the children to eat. Collect and **wash** the seeds. Let the children glue the seeds to a picture of a watermelon slice made from red and green construction paper.

Wear

Help the children make a list of things they like to **wear**.

Weather

Talk about different types of **weather** and have the children keep a weather chart.

Weigh

Show the children how to use a scale. Have them **weigh** several different types of items, including themselves. Record the **weights** on a chart. Do any two or more children weigh exactly the same number of pounds?

Wheelbarrows/Wagons

Let the children fill, push or pull **wheelbarrows** and **wagons**.

Wheels

Have the children make a list of things that have **wheels**.

Whistle

Provide an assortment of **whistles** and let the children blow them.

Wind Chime

Hang a **wind** chime in the classroom near an open **window** or door. Listen to the sounds as the **wind** blows it.

Wings

Instruct the children to pretend their arms are **wings** and flap them like a bird or glide like an airplane.

Winking

Have the children practice **winking**.

Winter

Make a list of things to do during the **winter** months.

Worms

Learn about **worms**. Place some worms in the sand table for exploration.

Wreath

Make a holiday or decorative **wreath** for the classroom. Use a heavy cardboard base for the wreath. Provide a variety of colorful materials to decorate the wreath including **wallpaper** scraps, glue and scissors. Add a **wire** to the back of the wreath for hanging.

Write

Write each child's name and phone number on a strip of paper. Laminate the strips and place them in the Library/Writing Center. Invite the children to **write** or trace their names and phone numbers. Use the strips again and again.

Other words that begin with the letter W:

These words may arise in naturally occurring conversations throughout the day/week. As you use these words, point out that they start with the letter "w" and write them on an index card to add to your word board.

waffles, **whipped** cream, **white** milk (foods)

Wednesday, **weekend** (day of the **week**)

wet, **wide**, **whole**, **warm** (concepts)

when, **where**, **who**, **why** (question words)

wood (blocks, **workbench**)

wrench (tool)

weather symbols!

Picture Cards

worm

watermelon

wishing well

walrus

web

watch

window

wagon

windmill

TF1432 Letter of the Week!

Word Cards

wallet	wallpaper
walnuts	watering can
whisk	whistle
worms	wooden spoon
wool	weights
wreath	wrench
welcome mat	wood
wheel	washboard

Trace and Write

Trace and write the letters. Color the picture.

Name

Uppercase W

1 2 3 4

W W W W W W W W

Lowercase w

1 2 3 4

w w w w w w

My Alphabet Book

Name

I am learning about the letter W w.
This is how I write it:

W W W

W W

Here are some words that start with the letter W w:

This is my picture of a _____.

Name

Letter Y

Letter Z

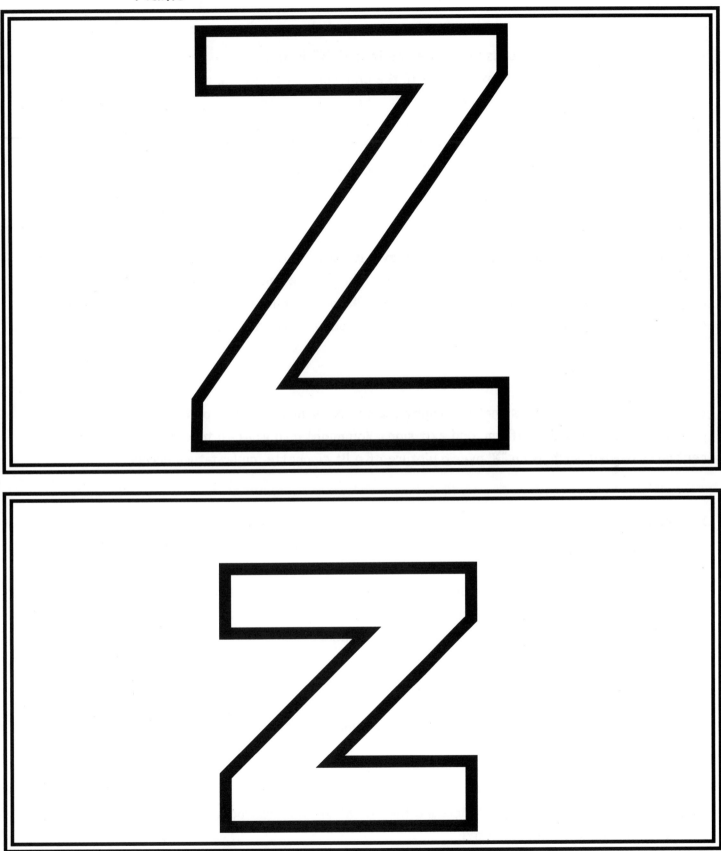

Ideas and Activities for the Letters:

X

Play a guessing game with words that have the letter "X" in them.

Give clues about each word below and see if the children can guess the words.

exit	ox	ax	box	fox	wax
fix	six	excellent	taxi	tuxedo	texture
saxophone	onyx	next	mix	experiment	extraordinary
exhibit	exercise	except	excuse		

X-rays

Ask a dentist, veterinarian, or physician if they have outdated **x-rays** to donate to your program. Hang the x-ray on a window so the sunlight will highlight the teeth/bones. Talk to the children about x-rays and why you might have an x-ray. Talk to the children about what doctors, dentists, and vets do with x-rays. Encourage children to talk about times they may have had an x-ray.

"X" Symbol

Discuss the different places that one might see an "X" symbol. Display pictures of railroad crossing, traffic guard's uniform, and exit sign. You might also want to talk about signs restricting certain activities, such as an "X' over a picture of a lit cigarette, or left-turn arrow.

Xylophone

Play musical chairs with a **xylophone**. Select a leader to play the xylophone and then suddenly stop playing while the children each find a chair. In the classic musical chairs game, a chair is removed between each playing of the music and the child without a chair is asked to sit off to the side. For younger children, leave all of the chairs in place and have all of the children play for the entire game. Invite the children to take turns being the leader.

Yams

With the children, peel, cook and eat **yams** for a **yummy** treat.

Yardstick

Measure things with a **yardstick**. Measure the height of the classroom door, the classroom floor, the teacher's desk, or the play yard.

Year

Use a calendar. Ask the children to count how many months/days are in one **year**?

Yellow

Make a **yellow** collage. Provide yellow scraps of **yarn,** pom poms, cellophane, cupcake holders, pipe cleaners, twist ties, paper, etc. Eat yellow foods for snack time, such as corn muffins, bananas, yellow cake, lemon **yogurt**. Make lemonade for a special drink.

Yesterday

During a morning circle time activity, ask the children to remember what happened **yesterday**. Write their responses on a large sheet of paper.

Yoga

Teach the children some simple **yoga** stretches.

Z

Play a guessing game with words that have the letter "Z" in them. Give clues about each word below and see if the children can guess the words.

pizza	breezy	dozen	wizard	waltz	apologize
freeze	magazine	squeeze	sneeze	size	razor
lizard	appetizer	nozzle	frozen	puzzle	prize

Zebra

Zebras have stripe patterns that are like human fingerprints- "unique." The stripes blend in with their surroundings and offer protection from predators. Using a marker, have the children draw black stripes on a zebra pattern.

Zero

Look for "0's" in license plates and on mailboxes or buildings. Roll clay to make a **zero**.

Zigzag

Copy a **zigzag** pattern and demonstrate to the children how to cut along a zigzag line. Have the children cut with pinking shears to make zigzags.

Zoo

Help the children make a list of **zoo** animals. Let them pretend to be zoo animals. They can walk like a chimpanzee, roar like a lion, walk like an elephant, hop like a kangaroo, stretch like a giraffe, etc. Look for more interesting ideas and information in the Early Childhood Thematic Book "Zoo Animals," Teacher's Friend Publications, 2001.

Other words that begin with the letters X,Y,Z:

These words may arise in naturally occurring conversations throughout the day/week. As you use these words, point out that they start with the letters "x, y, and z" and write them on index cards to add to your word board.

yes (response)

yo-yo (toy)

yummy (related to food)

zip, zipper (dressing)

zip code (on letters/addresses)

zodiac (signs)

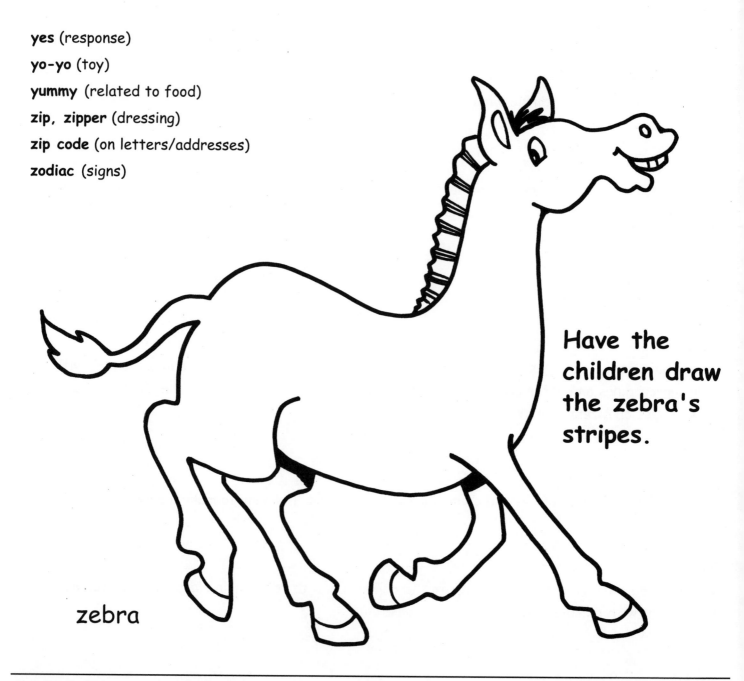

Have the children draw the zebra's stripes.

zebra

Picture Cards

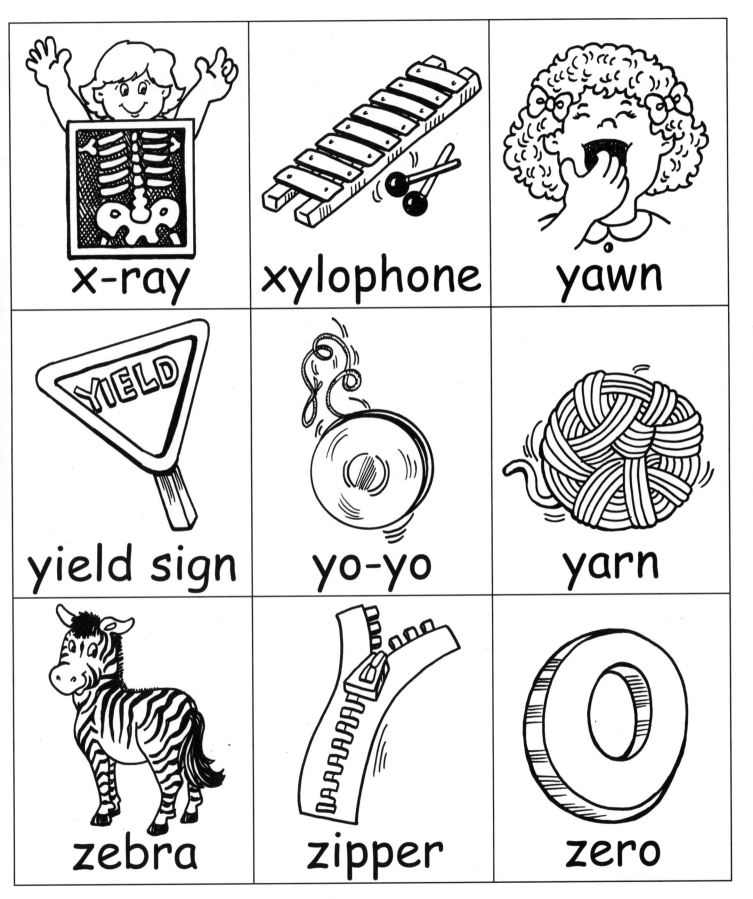

x-ray

xylophone

yawn

yield sign

yo-yo

yarn

zebra

zipper

zero

TF1432 Letter of the Week!

Word Cards

x-ray	xylophone
yardstick	yarn
yo-yo	yellow
yam	yogurt
yeast	school zone sign
zucchini	zebra
zinnia	zipper

Trace and write the letters. Color the picture.

Name

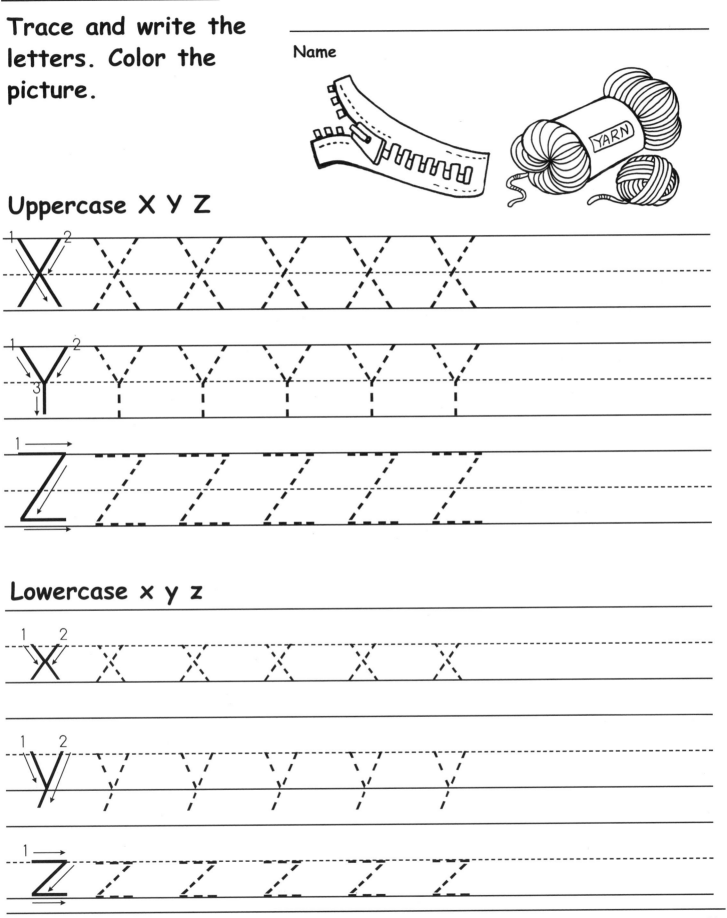

Uppercase X Y Z

Lowercase x y z

My Alphabet Book

Name

I am learning about the letter X x. This is how I write it:

Here are some words that start with the letter X x:

This is my picture of a _____ .

Name

I am learning about the letter Y y.
This is how I write it:

Here are some words that start with the letter Y y:

This is my picture of a _____ .

My Alphabet Book

Name

I am learning about the letter Z z. This is how I write it:

Here are some words that start with the letter Z z:

This is my picture of a _____.

Show-and-Tell Letter Home to Parents!

Dear Families,

We are learning about the letter ___ and the sound that it makes. We will be having Show-and-Tell on _____ .

Please assist your child in finding one item at home that begins with this letter and help him or her bring it to school to share.

Thank you for your help!

_____

- -

Letter Home to Parents!

Dear Families,

We are learning about the letter _____ and the sound that it makes. Here are a few ideas of how you can reinforce the important things your child is learning at school:

_____

_____

_____

_____

_____

Thank you for your help!

_____

Learning at Home!

There are many ways you can encourage your child at home to develop thinking skills and to reinforce what he or she is learning at school. Here are a few ideas:

Read to your child every day – Ask your child what the story is about. Ask your child to tell you his or her favorite part of the story. Encourage your child to tell you the story.

Look at family photos – Ask your child to identify the people in the pictures. Encourage him or her to remember what happened the day the photo was taken.

Make a grocery list – Ask your child to think of things that your family needs to purchase. Let him or her help you write the item on a list.

Identify signs you see – Talk about the signs you see, such as stop signs, exit signs, school crossing signs, etc. Tell him or her how signs help us to be safe. Encourage your child to identify specific colors and letters in the signs.

Write a story together – Encourage your child to tell you a story while you write it down. Help them recognize that the story has a beginning, middle and end. Ask your child to draw a picture of his or her story. Keep the stories in a notebook for your child to have and read as his or her own story book.

Setting the table – Ask your child to count how many people will be eating. Count the number of plates, utensils, etc. Fold napkins into rectangles, triangles.

Wash dishes together – Point out which dishes are "largest" and "smallest." Encourage your child to help wash specific dishes "first" or "last."

Sort clothes or toys – Show your child how to sort and fold clothes. Let him or her help you sort by color or type (socks, t-shirts, underwear, etc.). With your help, ask your child to organize their toys. Example: "Let's put your stuffed animals in the toy box and your books on the shelf."

Put away groceries – Encourage your child to help you sort items that need to be refrigerated and those that go in the cupboard. Let your child smell and feel fruit and vegetables. Ask your child, "What do you think is in this can or box?"

Cook simple foods – Ask your child to help you pop popcorn, prepare a sandwich, make a salad, scramble eggs, bake cookies, etc. Question them to think about what order things should be done and to notice how things change, feel and taste.

Listen to music or view television together – Ask your child to sing and clap to the music or help you make up a song. Watch television programs with your child and talk about the subject matter and encourage your child to ask questions. (Always make sure that the music, movies, and television programs you view with your child are appropriate.)

Index of Topical Words by Center (Interest Area)

Note: Many of the words or themes in this book can be associated with two or more centers. You may use your own discretion in deciding which center best applies to the appropriate topic.

Arts and Crafts Center:

aluminum foil, angle, artist, bank, banner, bead, blue, bricks, bug, chalk, corn, cut, delivery van, dragon, empty, fan, feet, fish, fold, gift, gold/gray/green, head, heart, igloo, menu, mosaic, napkin ring, nature, necklace, neon, newspaper, octagon, orange, ornament, pig, quarter, Queen Anne's lace, quilt, red, ribbon, snip, sole, stencil, tape, tiles, velour, vase, violets, walrus, watermelon, wreath, yellow, zigzag

Blocks and Building Center:

airport, automobile, bridge, build, construction, golf, jeep/jet, map, pyramids, river, signs, tools, towers, tubes, vehicles

Cooking and Nutrition Center:

appetizers, apples, apricot, bagel, banana, barbecue, bread, breakfast, buffet, butter, cafeteria, cake, chopsticks, clam, cookies, coupons, cube, eat, eggs, grandparent, grate, groceries, half, ice cream, iced tea, Italy, jack-o-lantern, jelly, jiggle, juice, kiwi, knife, lemon, lunch, meal, nachos, oatmeal, omelets, pancakes, pizza, produce party, quiche, raisins, recipe cards, refrigerator, salad, shake, snacks, table, tacos, umbrella, utensils, vegetables, yams

Dramatic Play Center:

baker, barber, camera, carpenter, clown, doctor, dolls, ears/eyes, glasses, hat, jacket, kayak, king, menu, mirror, picnic, polka dots, queen, repair shop, restaurant, scarf, telephone, tent, undress, uniform, veterinary, wallet

General Activities: (circle/group time, vocabulary/language development, social/ emotional development, self-help skill development)

aardvark, acrobat, actor, address, afraid, alike, angry, antler, armor, astronaut, attic, auditorium, baby, backwards, bag, bears, beaver, bedtime, bedroom, boa constrictor, boat, bones, brave, breathe, brush, butcher, calendar, camel, cardinal, cartoon, carnival, chores, city, clap, clothes, clouds, collect, cow, cry, dentist, different, dinosaurs, dogs, elephant, emotions, Eskimo, exit, face, family, farm, fire, flag, forest, frighten, giggle, giraffe, grow, grownup, hair, hands, hard, hello, hero, hibernate, hole, holiday, home, hospital, hot, iguana, insects, invention, janitor, job, jockey, kangaroo, kennel, kitchen, koala, Laundromat, left, lions, litter, living room, lizard, mail, manners, mayor, mechanic, morning, name, negotiate, neighbor, nephew, new, news, nickname, nighttime, noun, nurse, octopus, old, pairs, paper, partridge, people, pig, please, Pledge of Allegiance, police officer, principal, prize, quiet, rearrange, recall, reflection, relax, routine, scavenger hunt, sea, shepherd, snakes, snapping, snow, sparrow, sports, tails, television, unicycle, upset, vacation, ventriloquist, wand, wart, water, wear, wheels, winking, winter, yesterday, x-ray, "x" symbol, zebra, zoo

---

Library/Writing Center:

album, alphabet, atlas, aunt, author, avenue, branch, card, cross, dad, diamond, dictionary, end, envelope, initials, journal, knee, letters, license plates, mother, paperclip, postcards, thank you, tortoise, trace, treasure trunk, typewriter, uncle, UPC, write, x, z

Math and Manipulatives Center:

arm, balance, bean, birthday, bolts, boy, button, chain, cube, curly, degrees, dialing, dice, dollar, dozen, deck of cards, eight, funnel, gallon, height, hundred, jar, jigsaw puzzle, lacing, length, march, material, mitten, nail, nickel, nine, numbers, nuts, one, pea pods, pegboards, penny, pound, present, puzzle, quart, rice, rolling pin, scale, schedule, shape, spin, sponges, stairs, stand, string, tallest, tic tac toe, time, vote, walnut, weigh, yardstick, year, zero

Music and Movement Center:

accordion, action, ball, balloon, band, bare feet, beat, body parts, bucket, bugle, crab, dance, drum, exercise, gallop, guitar, hoop, horn, instruments, jog, jumping jacks, kick, kite, ladle, launch, leg, limbo, maraca, march, monkey, music, noisemaker, nylon, obstacle course, orchestra, outdoors, painter, parachute, piano, record, ride, scarecrow, slippers, soccer balls, sounds, stomp, swing, tambourine, tennis, throw, tiptoe, trumpet, ukulele, under, voice, walk, waltz, wheelbarrow, whistle, wings, xylophone, yoga

Science Center:

acorn, aquarium, breezy, bubble, bulb, candy cane, carnation, caterpillar, circle, dirt, Earth, experiment, fabric, flashlight, float, flower, fly, freeze, garbage, garden, globe, grasshopper, hamster, herbs, ice, incense, kaleidoscope, ladybug, log, magnet, melt, moss, mud, net, nose, odor, pepper, periscope, pet, petal, prism, pussy willow, rocks, roots, rough, round, scents, seeds, shadow, sky, tadpole, texture, toothbrush, traffic safety rules, volcano, watering can, weather, wind chime, worms

Transition Activity Ideas:

crab, curly, freckles, girl, jumping jacks, quack, roar, scratch, stair, stomp, tiptoe, wand, wings, winking